58 LINES

Theories of linear improvisation for the evolving guitarist

RODNEY JONES with ALEX LEVINE

Online Audio www.melbay.com/31209MEB

Cover art & design by Miles Okazaki
Photos courtesy of Rachel Jones

Exclusive Sales Agent: Mel Bay Publications, Inc.
WWW.MELBAY.COM

TABLE OF CONTENTS

Foreword by Miles Okazaki 6
Preface and Acknowledgments by Rodney Jones 8
Introduction and Acknowledgments by Alex Levine 10

How to Read the Fingerings 13

Line 1 14
Blues in F - Audio 2 & 3 - shifting while retaining shape, covering range
Line 2 17
Blues in F - Audio 4 & 5 - nine-note figure, reorienting figures, V-I idea
Line 3 20
Blues in F - Audio 6 & 7 - two notes per string, interlocking triads, pivot points
Line 4 23
Blues in F - Audio 8 & 9 - picking exercises, moveable cells
Line 5 28
Blues Minor - Audio 10 & 11 - descending chromatics, chromatic enclosure, Miles chromatics
Line 6 31
G Minor Blues - Audio 12 & 13 - fourths/fifths cells, triads in whole tones
Line 7 34
Darn That Dream - Audio 14 & 15 - seven-note and five-note figures, legato chromatics
Line 8 39
A Minor Vamp - Audio 16 & 17 - connecting chromatics, arpeggios, and scalar fragments
Line 9 40
Blues in F - Audio 18 & 19 - using only first and third fingers, using familiar shapes to get different combinations
Line 10 43
G Minor Blues - Audio 20 & 21 - shifting mid-idea, using the physical framework of cells, phrase length variation, conversation
Line 11 46
Impressions - Audio 22 & 23 - arpeggios in four and five-note groupings, departing/returning to home tonality, identifying cells and phrases
Line 12 50
It Could Happen To You - Audio 24 & 25 - chord voicings as physical frames and moveable figures, ii-V-i idea, arpeggios applied on different chords
Line 13 52
Jeannine - Audio 26 & 27 - minor seventh arpeggio using fingers one and four, structure of arpeggios
Line 14 54
Lover Man - Audio 28 & 29 - chromatic approach notes and enclosures, ghost notes
Line 15 57
Blues Minor - Audio 30 & 31 - same shape played with different fingering, broken chromatics, rhythmic spacing, breath, symmetrical ♯9 shape
Line 16 60
A Night in Tunisia - Audio 32 & 33 - rhythmic groupings of five, six, and seven, descending chromatics

Line 17 63
Willow Weep For Me - Audio 34 & 35 - ghost notes, seven-note short/long permutations
Line 18 67
Giant Steps - Audio 36 & 37 - moving cells through changes, V-I phrases through changes
Line 19 72
Days of Wine and Roses - Audio 38 & 39 - combining bebop language with descending fourths
Line 20 75
Giant Steps - Audio 40 & 41 - additive rhythms, isolating and applying rhythmic phrases
Line 21 78
Softly, as in a Morning Sunrise - Audio 42 & 43 - exploring alternative fingerings
Line 22 81
Blues in F - Audio 44 & 45 - minor triads in minor thirds, three-note device falling back through the beat
Line 23 83
Blues in F - Audio 46 & 47 - sonic trickery, using familiar phrases in unexpected ways
Line 24 86
Blues in F - Audio 48 & 49 - tritone substitution, melodic figures from physical chord shapes
Line 25 89
D Minor Blues - Audio 50 & 51 - shifts guided by individual melodic cells
Line 26 92
Blues in F - Audio 52 & 53 - chromatic enclosures targeting chord tones, moving between rhythmic strata
Line 27 96
Vamp in B♭ Minor - Audio 54 & 55 - fifths and fourths concept, Arthur Blythe
Line 28 99
D Minor Blues - Audio 56 & 57 - phrasing with pentatonics, changing fingers to play one note
Line 29 102
D Minor Blues - Audio 58 & 59 - hammer-ons and dynamics, conversational phrases
Line 30 105
Softly, as in a Morning Sunrise - Audio 60 & 61 - sliding, the impact of fingerings on the directionality of ideas
Line 31 107
Blues Minor - Audio 62 & 63 - rhythmic punctuation, grammar
Line 32 109
Blues Minor - Audio 64 & 65 - patterns of varying lengths, rhythmic structure
Line 33 112
Blues Minor - Audio 66 & 67 - dominant to tonic resolution, minor tonalities moving in different intervals
Line 34 115
Blues in F - Audio 68 & 69 - blues language, articulation, singing quality
Line 35 118
Blues in F - Audio 70 & 71 - 1235 shape and variations
Line 36 121
Impressions - Audio 72 & 73 - whole-tone figure
Line 37 124
Rhythm Changes - Audio 74 & 75 - triple feel, scalar idea filled in with chromatics, fourths as a framework for expanding ideas
Line 38 127
Impressions - Audio 76 & 77 - directionalism

Line 39 130
F Minor Blues - Audio 78 & 79 - shifting tonalities, chord on every beat
Line 40 133
Blues Minor - Audio 80 & 81 - C minor and B♭ major triads over F minor
Line 41 136
D Minor Vamp - Audio 82 & 83 - George Benson influence, slide/interval leap to an adjacent string
Line 42 140
Blues in G - Audio 84 & 85 - fundamental diatonic sequences and arpeggios, minor seventh chords a major third apart
Line 43 143
So What - Audio 86 & 87 - descending chromatic, shifting tonalities while keeping the same fingering
Line 44 146
Softly, as in a Morning Sunrise - Audio 88 & 89 - ascending C minor, descending B minor
Line 45 148
Softly, as in a Morning Sunrise - Audio 90 & 91 - reaching out of position for a note
Line 46 151
Unit 7 - Audio 92 & 93 - fourths a whole tone apart, triad permutations
Line 47 154
Speak Low - Audio 94 & 95 - triplets grouped in twos, ghost notes
Line 48 157
Lover Man - Audio 96 & 97 - G minor tetrachord, retaining the same fingering through the range, scale fragments in various note groupings
Line 49 160
Little Sunflower - Audio 98 & 99 - building and expanding phrases from a rhythmic idea
Line 50 162
Blues in F - Audio 100 & 101 - shifting, directionalism
Line 51 165
D Minor Blues - Audio 102 & 103 - arpeggios with different numbers of notes, changing direction, delayed resolution
Line 52 168
Blues Minor - Audio 104 & 105 - musical sentences, structure from shifts in position, tonality, or rhythm, melodic shapes in tritones
Line 53 172
Little Sunflower - Audio 106 & 107 - four-over-three, whole-tone device
Line 54 175
Impressions - Audio 108 & 109 - two notes per string, chromatics cells, repeated notes on different strings
Line 55 178
Summertime - Audio 110 & 111 - sense of direction, target points, chromatic enclosure
Line 56 181
Speak Low - Audio 112 & 113 - arpeggios with note groupings of five and four
Line 57 184
Speak Low - Audio 114 & 115 - descending chromatics into chord tones
Line 58 187
Blues in F - Audio 116 & 117 - three-finger technique, repeated note on the same string with different fingers

Alex Levine and Rodney Jones

FOREWORD

"It can only be caught, not taught." This is a phrase that Rodney Jones would often use to describe the intangible details of a musical phrase or concept that escapes the ability of language to describe how it works or why it sounds compelling. The ability to catch the thing in question depends on the student's capacity to listen closely with an open mind and find something previously hidden from their perception. In this style of passing down information from one generation to the next, the job of the teacher is not to impose their method or pedagogical system but to train the student to think in a way that will sustain their creativity and nourish their individuality. The method of training can come in many forms, but with Mr. Jones, the delivery system is most clearly encapsulated in mysterious improvised melodic sentences. What he would call "hip lines."

I began studying with Rodney Jones in 1997. He became the most important mentor in my life, and remains the touchstone for my approach to music and the guitar. I met Alex Levine in 2012, and through his studies with me, he became familiar with Rodney's approach, eventually contacting him directly to go to the source. This process is ongoing - in my early days, Rodney introduced me to his mentor Bruce Johnson. He didn't do this for anyone - it required me to demonstrate a dedication to the craft that warranted the generational connection. For years we talked about making the "hip lines book," an instructional book that would contain transcriptions of his spontaneous playing and some kind of explanation of what was going on. But during this time, I was mostly concerned with trying to catch the vibe, feel, and spirit of his playing and not sweating all the details. I figured that the analytical work might be a job for someone else, and it turns out that Mr. Levine was up to the task.

In this book, Alex Levine has produced a truly unique study, providing a look under the hood of a specific approach to creative improvisation on the guitar. The evolution of this language involves the lineage of melodic guitar playing that grows from the roots of Charlie Christian, Grant Green, Wes Montgomery, Kenny Burrell, and Barney Kessel, and continues in the later 20th century through Nathen Page, Ted Dunbar, Jack Wilkins, Bruce Johnson, and above all, the grandmaster George Benson. In this tradition, the raw data (the notes and rhythms) are not the whole story - this information can only pass from musician to listener through the intentionality of articulation and feel. For this reason, as in learning any language, it's essential to listen to the source material as sound, using the book as a guide to understanding the architecture involved.

The contribution that Alex has made in his notes on each line is enormous. In his analyses, he shows that the line itself is not the thing but only one manifestation of many possible versions of that thing. He breaks each line down into essential elements and recombines them into exercises and conceptual studies. The underlying truth to this approach is that, in studying master improvisers, our goal is not to play their material verbatim but to imitate it and then extrapolate it through the filter of our own personality. You are not going to play Rodney's lines better than Rodney. Still, you can expand the potential of your playing through the internalization of his melodic language, and an understanding of the underlying grammar that the lines are built from.

In working my way through the lines, it occurred to me that there are certain questions people may ask. So I'll wrap up this foreword with my opinion on these topics in a question-and-answer format.

Q: Why is there no tablature?
A: There are a few reasons. The first is that tablature will not help, and in fact will hinder, a guitarist's ability to read staff notation. Guitarists' reputation in this area is bad enough, and we should be taking steps to educate ourselves. Secondly, since the lines are on standard staff notation, musicians on other instruments can read them, which extends the usefulness of the book in general. But the more important thing is that, with Rodney Jones' lines, the secret to the articulation often lies in the fingering (a piece of information absent in tablature) and the rhythmic phrasing (which tab is bad at). There are very subtle choices being made all the time for fingerings that are not necessarily "by the book" in the service of hipper articulation, rhythmic feel, and dynamics. The combination of fingering markings with Roman

numeral position markings gives the reader all the information they need to put the right fingers in the right places, and the staff notation shows the rhythms in the most efficient way. My recommendation for a workflow would be something like this: listen to the sample, learn and memorize the fingering, go back and play along with the sample and imitate the articulation, move on to exercises and analysis, then come up with your own stuff based on the concepts at hand.

Q: Why are the samples from practice tapes and live gigs with rough audio rather than studio recordings?
A: Rodney Jones has a wonderful discography to select from, but these tapes show him in practice mode, where the real work is done. Studio recordings present a polished version of the performer, but what we want to know is how to get from point A to point B, to peek inside the practice room and hear what kind of process is used by master musicians. To hear Rodney's compositions and arrangements, his interactions with a band, and his tone recorded with high-quality microphones, go to the studio recordings. But to hear the work done to get to that point, go to the practice tapes. For these examples, Alex has combed through hundreds of hours of video. In many cases, Rodney plays for more than an hour on a single tune. You could drop the needle anywhere and find a hip line, so treat these examples not as a "best of", but more like a curated collection of snapshots of a moving target.

Q: Where are the chords and harmony - isn't that important on guitar?
A: Yes, chords are important on the guitar, but that may be a topic for another book. The study of melody is the study of chords with one note. Rodney is a great practitioner of chordal work on the guitar, but this is a focused study on linear playing. A deep dive into one topic is always better than a superficial survey.

Q: What makes these lines hip?
A: Let me give you a short list of examples: combining hard swing with abstract vocabulary (line 6), using ghost notes to provide rhythmic drive (line 8), flow and accents at a fast tempo (line 11), rubato phrasing and lyricism on a ballad (line 12), extreme melodic detail in a bebop context (line 16), using a few ingredients to get a lot of results (line 25), breaking ankles (line 31), heavy blues (line 34), mixing duple and triple (line 37), invisible position shifting (line 38, 50), triplets with ghosts (line 47), call and response with contrary motion (line 52), false fingering (line 54), George Benson extended (lines 7, 20, 29, 33, 41, and many others). These are not beginner concepts. They are the details achieved through a lifetime of work on articulation and precision in the execution of musical ideas. In the beginning stages of learning a language, the student is just trying to get the right words in the right order. But to have the phrases flow and communicate like a native speaker, the student needs to master articulation, rhythm, and feel. In my opinion, this is what the hipness of these lines has to teach us.

Q: Who is Rodney Jones anyway?
A: If you bought this book, then you probably know. But one thing to understand about Mr. Jones is that all of the technical work that he has done is only in service to make music with a spiritual impact. His music is as soulful as it gets, and its purpose is to spread love and connection between people. His generosity is evident in the way that he shares information about his work and his personal interactions with the people in his life (as Alex and I have been lucky enough to know). It's understood that technique can't be a pursuit in itself that leads to any kind of spiritual fulfillment, but it's the mastery of the craft that allows you to have limitless expression on the instrument and freedom from the obstacles that block continual personal growth. I'm very happy that this book has finally been made, both for Rodney and for the many guitarists who will have their heads turned around by it. So, that being said, I'll sign off with another Rodney-ism: "That's my story, and I'm sticking to it."

Miles Okazaki, Brooklyn, 2024

PREFACE

Welcome to *58 Lines*. This book is deeply personal to me. It contains a body of work and exploration that has been a lifetime in the making. It is intended to be a guidebook, a window, and a portal into a way of playing the guitar and building lines and exercises that, to my knowledge, has never been explored in this way.

Take your time with what is presented here. It is a lot. I suggest that you loosely play through the lines, practice along with the recordings, and see how it feels, where it leads?

These lines and the way of playing them have the potential to transform what you play and believe is possible to play. The magic sauce of it all is to Rinse and Repeat these lines and exercises until they become familiar to you. Applying them to tunes that you know and building your own ideas around them will greatly expedite your progress and skill.

Alex has done an amazing job organizing and explaining each line's theory and premise. Read what he says about the lines and the exercises and weigh it carefully. There are many hundreds of hours behind the lines and his expounding upon them.

58 Lines is intended to be a part of your musical journey and inquiry. I do not say that it is the only way to play or the only thing that you should study. It is, however, an invaluable tool to explore the ocean of sound and the possibilities of the guitar in jazz improvisation.

I want to acknowledge the brilliant musician and guitarist Miles Okazaki for his expertise, skill, and love, which he so generously shared in the preparation of this book. His unique genius and understanding of music and what lies behind the music is imbued throughout this text. Make sure to read his foreword, as it provides deep insight and wisdom.

Without my friend Alex Levine there is no *58 Lines* book. His care, encouragement, and personal work is the data center for everything in this book. I conceived it and played it. Alex manifested it and collated it into the form that you hold in your hand. He is the engine behind manifesting the *58 Lines*. I could not be more grateful to him and for his friendship.

There are many friends who lent their wisdom and views in playing through much of this material. Beth Marlis, the brilliant guitarist and educator, provided deep wisdom and insight. David Rosenthal, Bobby Sexton, and Brayden Bradford all played through the lines and helped refine their presentation.

I thank my wife, Rachel, for listening to countless hours of me practicing and developing this vocabulary.

I thank my daughters, Leana, Serena, Laura, and Cara, and my grandchildren, Miran, Laura, Ava, and Oliver, for opening my heart so wide. I love them beyond all measure.

None of this would be possible were it not for the love and genius of John Coltrane who pioneered musical freedom and the spirit of exploration.

I thank McCoy Tyner who is a huge influence and inspiration.

I thank my most important guitar teacher, Bruce Johnson, who was the first one to show me what is possible and encourage me to find my own way.

Sri Harold Klemp and the ECK Masters of the Vairagi. Without their guidance and presence, I would never have found the "Notes that want to be played."

Finally, it was, and is, my love for and gratitude for the life of my sweet granddaughter Ava Jane that was the motivation to keep going. Each morning, around 5:00 AM, I would get up and practice and play to honor and celebrate her. This book is my love letter to her.

This book is now my love letter to you.

To quote a famous line, "The last pages in the book are for you."

With gratitude and appreciation - Rodney

A Special Note of Thanks:

There are many people who make a book like this possible. I want to offer thanks and gratitude to William Bay. He is responsible for so many wonderful books shared with the world from Mel Bay, and those books have changed the lives of many musicians. He has been a constant supporter of my book ideas, and without him, *58 Lines* would not have been possible.

I also want to thank the wonderful staff at Mel Bay: Sharon Feldman, Joanne Wiggins, Julie Wakefield, and Josh Buck. Their brilliance, skill, and expertise behind the scenes resonate throughout every aspect of this book.

To contact Rodney and for information about Rodney's jazz guitar courses, email jazzguitarscholars@
gmail.com

INTRODUCTION

The process that led to this book began with a question posed to me by Rodney Jones in 2021. What if you learned one line per week for a year? How would your playing evolve? What tools and techniques would you discover and develop? Although the suggestion was open-ended as to the source of the lines, it was clear that I wanted to study Rodney's playing. It was a unique opportunity to follow one master musician for the year and be present to witness the daily evolution of his playing, the development of new ideas, the reemergence and furthering of old ideas, and the technical, artistic, and spiritual process. After one year, if I held to the goal of learning just one line per week, I would not only have fifty-two new lines in my vocabulary, but I would gain insight into what can be a mystifying and sometimes hidden aspect of music – practicing, the creative process and the technical work of developing as a guitarist.

Rodney Jones' mastery of the guitar and music is vast and multifaceted. He elevates any musical situation as a side musician and is one of the great accompanists. While building upon the foundation of recognizable influences, including George Benson, Nathen Page, Barney Kessel, Bruce Johnson, John Coltrane, and others, Rodney possesses a singular approach to improvisation that involves vocabulary and mechanical methodologies on the guitar that he has developed through his explorations. All of the lines in this book are presented through the distinctive lens through which Rodney views the music. Some are traceable to specific musicians or lineages, such as Dizzy Gillespie, George Benson, Wes Montgomery, Arthur Blythe, or Nathen Page, while others are more obscured in terms of their origins, having more to do with working out or expanding on a conceptual framework, musical device, or mechanical challenge.

Part of the benefit of learning one line per week was that my own shifting focus and musical goals were reflected in the line I selected to learn each week. The procedure for choosing a line was straightforward - listen to the recordings that Rodney was posting online of his daily practice sessions, then select a line that stood out to me in some way, whether it involved an idea or musical approach that I felt was missing from my vocabulary, something that baffled me in terms of guitar mechanics, something where my eyes couldn't believe my ears (or vice-versa), a particular harmonic situation that I wanted to figure out, a tune that I was working on, a rhythmic concept or way of phrasing that struck me, etc. Often, the line I chose was a direct response to different topics or suggestions that came up in my lessons and conversations with Rodney. While fifty-eight lines made it into this book, Rodney played countless lines that are equally great and worthy of study. The crucial factor was which line resonated with me and best served my musical journey at that moment. As Rodney says, "What is the note that wants to be played?" Because of the nature of Rodney's diverse musical interests and the vastness of his musical vocabulary, I believe that the fifty-eight lines represent a strong survey of approaches to linear improvisation and are a beneficial resource for any musician who is seeking to broaden their musical concept and skills as an improviser.

Focusing on just one line per week enabled particular attention to detail. So, in addition to learning the rhythms and pitches and the musical context in which a line was originally played, it was also important to me to understand how the ideas were executed, particularly the fingerings. In looking through the lines in this book, you will notice that no universal system or a single set of rules is used to select fingerings. Instead, many approaches are strategically deployed for different devices and musical situations. Rodney has developed a personal concept for determining fingerings based on criteria including sound, feel, phrasing, context, mindset, and physical preparedness at any given moment. While one approach to this material could be to learn the lines using whatever physical techniques you have become accustomed to, I highly suggest learning the material as played by Rodney. There are so many lessons in every choice, and the lifetime of experience and contemplation Rodney has put into the instrument provides a map to explore a multitude of musical ideas, ultimately leaving you with the freedom to choose how you want to play!

I do not suggest approaching this book as something you "read." Although you could easily play through all of the lines in this book in a matter of hours, you would be doing yourself a disservice to move through the material without giving your full attention to each line for an extended time. While taking a cursory glance through the material at the outset could give you a helpful overview of the types of lines you will find, it is unlikely to lead to significant development in your musicianship or creativity. Take your time with each line, exploring the possibilities offered, the mechanical challenges addressed, and the potential ways of building your musical approach using the concepts that emerge from the ideas. The notes and exercises supplement the lines and suggest ways of engaging with and learning from the material. They are examples of how you could build out your skills as a guitarist and improviser through in-depth study and experimentation. Use them as a guide, but don't fear treading "off path," searching for personal ways to develop the ideas and technical skills these lines suggest.

For me, much of the benefit in learning and practicing this material has come from repeating the lines over and over again, playing them so much that they have become a part of my musical identity. The more I repeated the lines themselves, the more freely I could apply the musical concepts and techniques embodied by the lines in my improvisations. Developing these ideas through analysis, exercises, and experimentation is supported by becoming deeply connected to the material itself. There is no shortcut to this process, only "rinsing and repeating," as Rodney says.

Why fifty-eight lines? While I set out to learn one line per week for one year, I decided to keep the project going for six more weeks after the year. One motivation for continuing beyond the initial goal was Rodney's reminder that often, we stop working on something too soon, just before yielding the most potent lessons and benefits. Sometimes, the most significant growth comes through pushing beyond what you thought was possible. In addition, it wasn't until after the halfway point of the "line-per-week" practice that Rodney suggested eventually turning this material into a book, and there were some specific musical devices and approaches that I knew I still hadn't documented.

Any student of Rodney must recognize that the research and development of his musical concept is constantly evolving and is truly a moving target. There is a continuum of devices and ideas that emerge at different times. Some become permanent fixtures of his musical language, and others recede into the ocean of sounds he draws from. This approach to creativity means going forward without fear of what you may leave behind in the process of searching for new ideas. Some musicians are tethered to ideas that have become familiar and well-rehearsed. The lines in this book are a reflection of a guitarist who is unafraid of taking risks and pushing boundaries. By looking closely at these lines and contemplating how they were developed, I hope you are inspired and encouraged to chart your own course, drawing on the spirit and wisdom Rodney has imparted through his musical explorations.

I believe that the work and musical language represented in this book are profound not only because of the brilliance and mastery of Rodney Jones as a guitarist but also because of the intention behind the notes. His greatness as a musician is matched by his kindness and generosity as a human being. He sets an example for all of us who are in pursuit of musical excellence. Beyond his artistry and commitment to music, Rodney is a positive force in the lives of those he loves and cares for, his family, friends, students, and community. I have benefited from Rodney's friendship, wisdom, and graciousness on both a personal and musical level. His mentorship has been a life-altering experience for me. It is a debt that can't be repaid, only paid forward. While love is at the core of the music represented in this book, make no mistake, as Rodney has said, "It takes what it takes." The work of reaching for the heights of expression offered by these lines is not to be taken lightly. Rodney has demonstrated that it can be done.

Alex Levine, New York City, 2024

To contact Alex and for questions/inquiries, email alexlevineguitar@gmail.com

ALEX LEVINE'S ACKNOWLEDGMENTS

My contributions to this book were only possible with many people's support, guidance, and input. I want to acknowledge the following:

My wife, Jing, for her unyielding support and belief in me, her love and encouragement, and her expert advice on design and visual concepts.

My family and especially my parents for their unconditional love and supporting me from the start.

Miles Okazaki for his example, lessons, and musical guidance, and for letting me into his process on numerous projects. My studies with Miles led me to eventually establish a connection with Rodney, who was instrumental in Miles' musical development. He has been extraordinarily supportive of this project, beginning with extensive practice sessions during which we studied some of the lines in this book. His insights into Rodney's playing were deeply illuminating. Miles' approach fundamentally informs how I view practice and musical research, and his influence is found throughout the observations and exercises in this book. In addition, Miles proofread the entire manuscript, providing crucial feedback and corrections, contributed a foreword for the book, and designed the front cover.

Noah Becker for his expert advice as a copyist, proofreading the lines and correcting notational errors.

Ben Rolston and Frances Ross for guidance on layout and design and excellent feedback on the notes and exercises.

Beth Marlis for reading through many iterations of the book, beginning with the first few lines and exercises, and providing indispensable feedback and insight.

David Rosenthal for providing valuable notes and challenging me to look at the material in new ways.

The entire community of guitarists in Rodney's Tune World and Line World groups for positive feedback, shared purpose, and camaraderie.

Ben Quachtran for looking through many of the notes and exercises as I was writing them, testing out concepts and devices, and giving me consistent feedback on the effectiveness of the material.

Geri Allen for pushing me to pursue a higher standard of musicianship and research and for her kindness, nurturing, and support during my first years in New York. Her projects focusing on the language of musicians, including Eric Dolphy, Herbie Hancock, McCoy Tyner, Cecil Taylor, and others, inspired my work for this book.

Henry Grimes for introducing me to new dimensions of creativity and focus through many hours of lessons and playing together, sharing his wisdom and genius.

Guitarists who have been important teachers, friends, mentors, and inspirations: Frank Portolese, Ray Ureña, Perry Hughes, and Steve Shepard.

Friends and colleagues who gave me additional feedback, talking through concepts and working out ideas: Yuma Uesaka, Marcus Elliot, Ian Finkelstein, Peyton Pleninger, Stefano Grasso, Russell Kranes, Andy Warren, and Michel Maurer.

Rodney Jones for entrusting me with this work.

HOW TO READ THE FINGERINGS

The fingerings in this book are represented with a notation system that uses numbers to indicate the finger that plays each note and Roman numerals to indicate the position on the fretboard. The digits refer to each finger (1 = index, 2 = middle, 3 = ring, 4 = pinky). The Roman numerals show the position on the fretboard based on the location of the first finger. Here is an example using a standard fingering for the C major scale in seventh position.

Here is another example using the C major scale played with two notes per string ascending and descending, which requires shifting positions.

Here is an example using the chromatic scale played with four notes per string.

Line 1

♩ = 220

Source: Blues in F

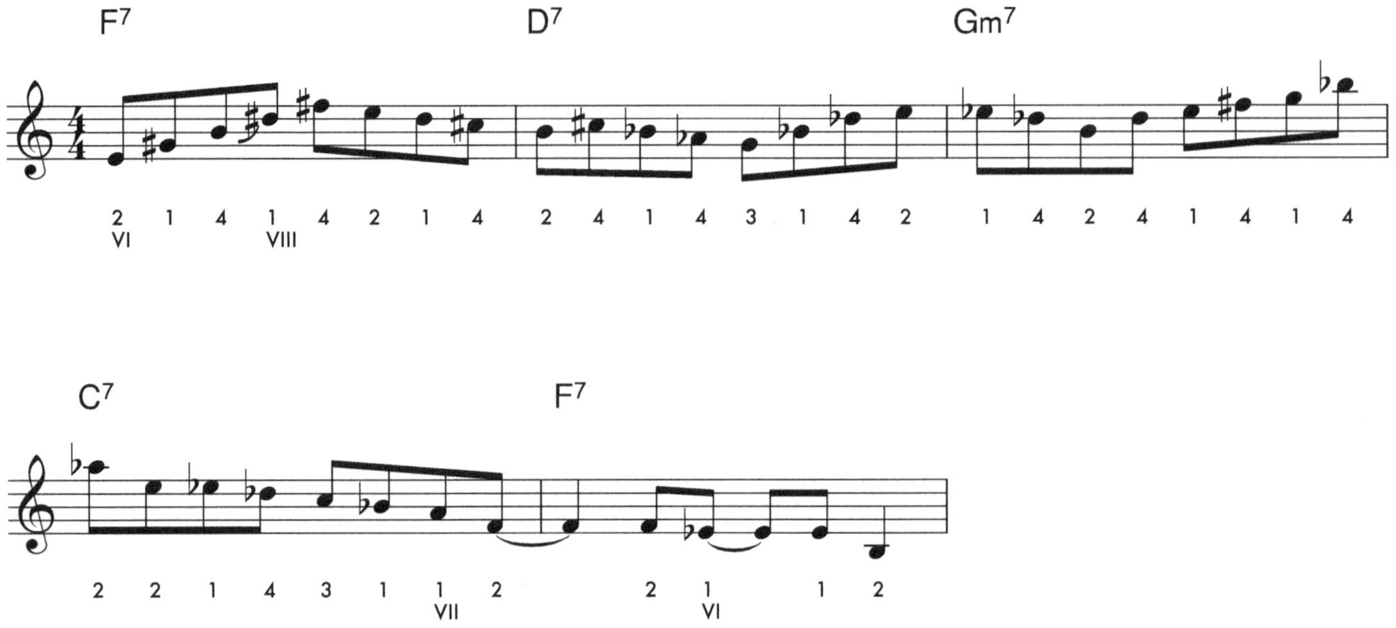

Line 1 Notes

Notice how the first phrase in this line includes a shift in position, retaining the same fingering to play two minor thirds a fifth apart.

Shifting creates a different flow than playing the idea in a single position on the instrument. There are many considerations when selecting fingerings, including tone, timbre, physical ease, note groupings, direction, and overall musical flow. The execution of an idea is informed by where it is coming from and where it is going.

The physical approach used in the phrase above is well-suited for covering a wide range on the guitar. Here are some example exercises expanding parts of the phrase through the range of the instrument.

The phrase repeats minor thirds a fifth apart. Experiment shifting minor thirds in different intervals, retaining the same fingering on each string. Here are some examples. Take note of the various types of chords generated by combining pairs of minor thirds in different intervallic relationships. Try playing these figures over different bass notes and observe how the harmonic implications change.

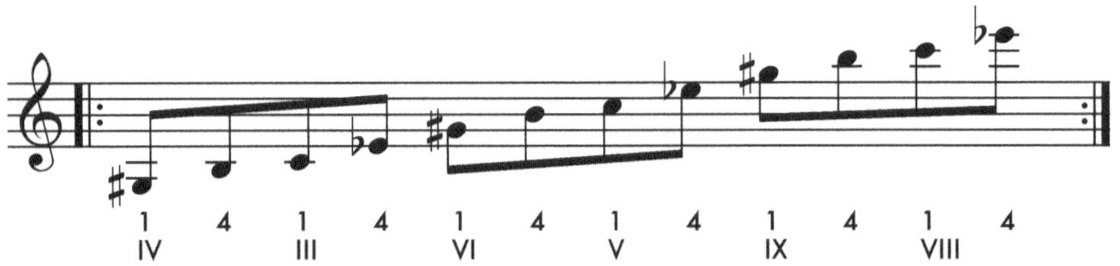

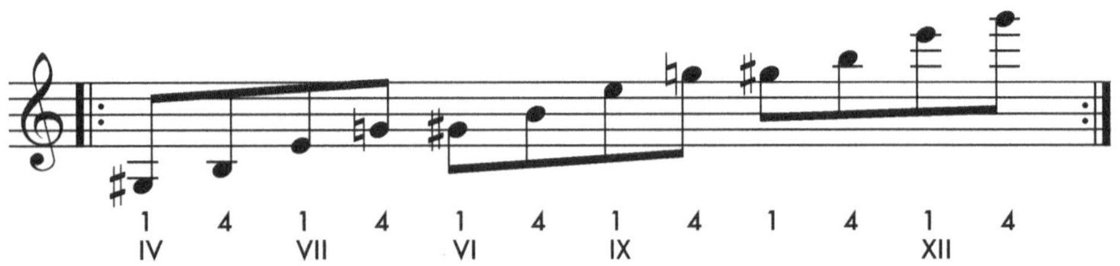

The additional examples below illustrate how this concept could be applied using other intervals. Also, explore using figures with more than two pitches on a single string. This approach to movement on the guitar offers a pathway to discovering new musical ideas and alternative ways of implementing devices already in your vocabulary.

Line 2

♩= 220

Source: Blues in F

Line 2 Notes

The first phrase of this line includes a nine-note melodic figure built off of a C minor tetrachord (C E♭ F G).

When repeated in a duple subdivision, this nine-note figure's orientation to the beat alternates between starting on the downbeat and upbeat. As an exercise, try looping the phrase to get a sense of how it feels starting on different parts of the beat and bar. Here is an example exercise moving the line down in half steps, cycling through all the possible orientations of the phrase in a measure of 4/4 in an eighth note subdivision.

For clarity, try counting aloud while playing the phrase, or use a clave or any repeating rhythmic figure to maintain awareness of how the phrase's placement changes.

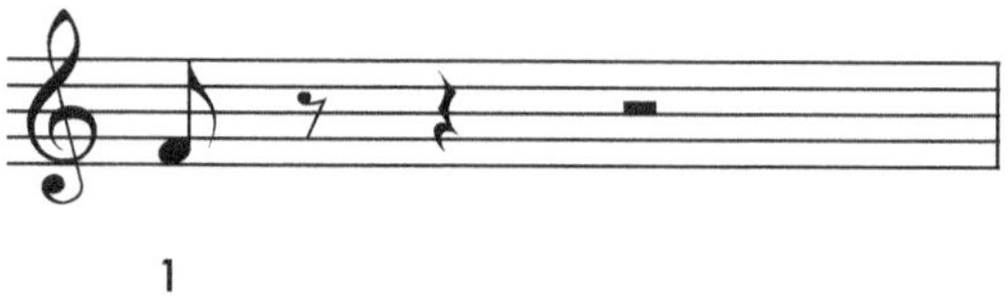

This phrase is a core cadential idea commonly played on a V-I or ii-V-I progression. It is built from two minor chords a half step apart. A fifth above the ii chord, and a half step above the V chord. In this case, G minor and F♯ minor 6. Many alternate fingerings could be applicable depending on the context of the idea. Practice it through the keys and in different octaves and string sets.

As an experiment, generate some variations using the same pitches and rhythms, altering the direction, order, or octave of parts of the phrase. Here are some example variations.

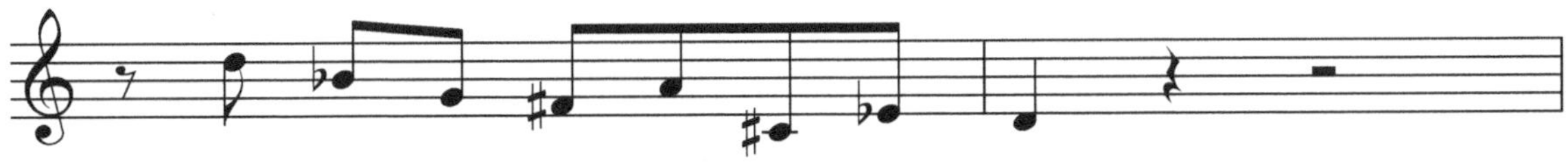

Line 3

♩ = 220

Source: Blues in F

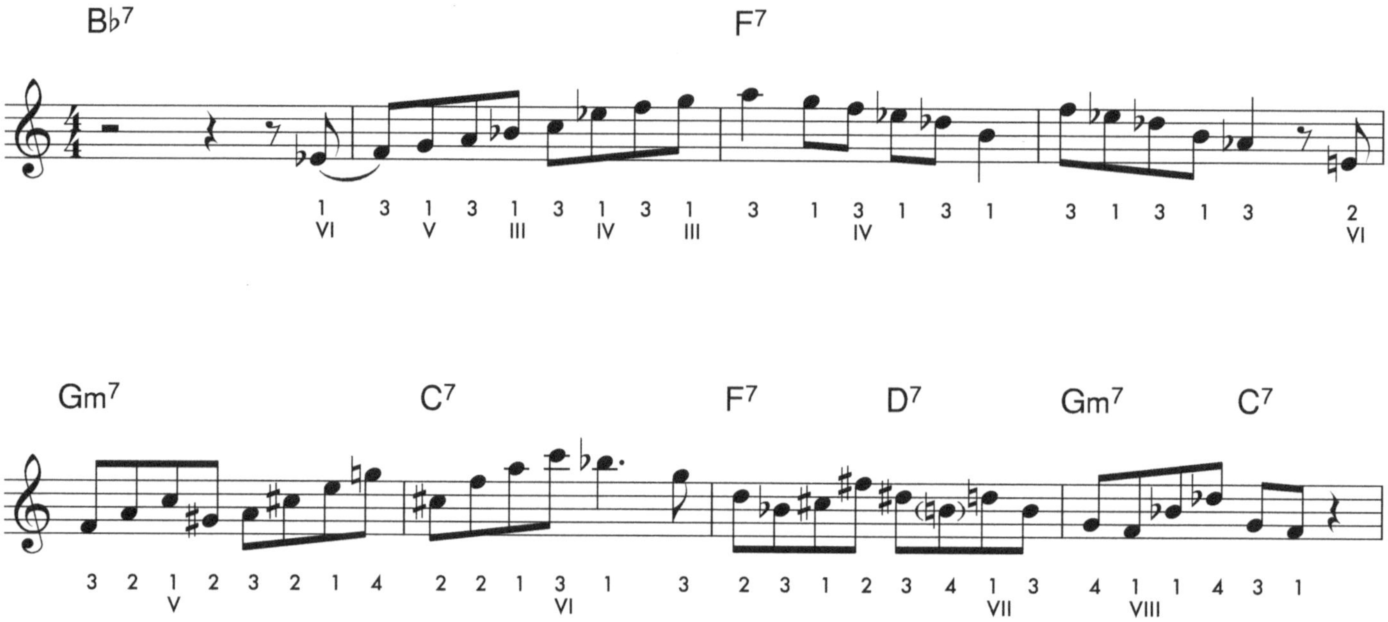

Line 3 Notes

Notice that the first phrase of this line, an F dominant figure, is played with only fingers 1 and 3, with two notes per string.

Consider different possible ways to play scales using only fingers 1 and 3. Here is an example fingering for the whole-tone scale.

Here is a potential fingering for the F Mixolydian scale using only fingers 1 and 3.

Apply this concept to any scale or melodic idea, limiting yourself to a given set of fingers or number of notes per string. Try using the same principle over a tune or a vamp. Working with a so-called "limiting" factor can focus your practice and give you greater insight into the materials already part of your musical vocabulary.

This phrase utilizes interlocking triads. Each successive triad shares one note with the previous triad. The common tone is also a pivot point where the line changes direction.

Explore ways to connect triads using a common tone as a pivot point. Here is an example exercise using interlocking major triads to extend the phrase from above. Apply the same concept using other types of triads and, more generally, using pivot points and common tones as a focusing element in your lines.

Line 4

♩ = 155

Source: Blues in F

Line 4 Notes

The first phrase of this line contains a cell that is useful for developing control of the pick.

Here is the basic cell, which can be altered or expanded in many ways. It can serve as a warm-up or technical exercise.

Practice the cell in various rhythmic feels and subdivisions, and experiment with different approaches to picking. Rather than providing any single solution to picking, using this compact, repeatable figure is a way to test and observe how the mechanics of any one approach works when applied to the cell and to measure your progress over time. Here are some examples of how the cell could be played in different rhythmic subdivisions.

This phrase is played by barring with the third finger to play a descending fourth from E♭ to B♭, creating a moveable cell that can be played with a limited range of motion.

Here is a variation on the cell using the same physical frame, barring with both the first and third fingers.

Here is another variation, omitting the lowest note, A♭, to make a three-note version of the cell. Again, bar the eighth fret to play B♭ and E♭.

As an exercise, practice each of these cells in various subdivisions to get a sense of how the three, four, and five-note figures can be situated rhythmically in different ways. This could be applied in any subdivision. Here is an example exercise playing each cell in eighth, triplet, and sixteenth note subdivisions.

Here is an exercise exploring some possible ways this cell could be moved around the instrument, ascending and descending through all the intervals within an octave. Notice that the physical shape is not adjusted to accommodate for the tuning of the G and B strings, so the resulting melodic formation is different on this string set. This is intentional, highlighting how a single physical shape can be used to generate different types of melodic figures.

1 3 1 3 3 1 3 1 3 3 1 3 1 3 3 1 3 1 3 3
VI IV VI VIII
1 3 1 3 3 1 3 1 3 3 1 3 1 3 3 1 3 1 3 3
VI VII VI
1 3 1 3 3 1 3 1 3 3 1 3 1 3 3 1 3 1 3 3
V IV
1 3 1 3 3 1 3 1 3 3 1 3 1 3 3 1 3 1 3 3
VI VII VI VIII
1 3 1 3 3 1 3 1 3 3 1 3 1 3 3 1 3 1 3 3
VI IX VI V
1 3 1 3 3 1 3 1 3 3 1 3 1 3 3 1 3 1 3 3
VI VII
1 3 1 3 3 1 3 1 3 3 1 3 1 3 3 1 3 1 3 3
VI VIII VI V
1 3 1 3 3 1 3 1 3 3 1 3 1 3 3 1 3 1 3 3
VI VII
1 3 1 3 3 1 3 1 3 3 1 3 1 3 3 1 3 1 3 3
VI VIII VI IX

Line 5

♩ = 262 Source: Blues Minor

Line 5 Notes

Notice how this phrase uses a descending chromatic line leading to a chromatic enclosure targeting the root of the chord, B♭ minor, to pivot to an upward-moving scalar idea.

As an exercise, use descending chromatics and a chromatic enclosure to target the chord's root, third and fifth. Practice connecting the chromatic device to various melodic ideas in the key of B♭ minor.

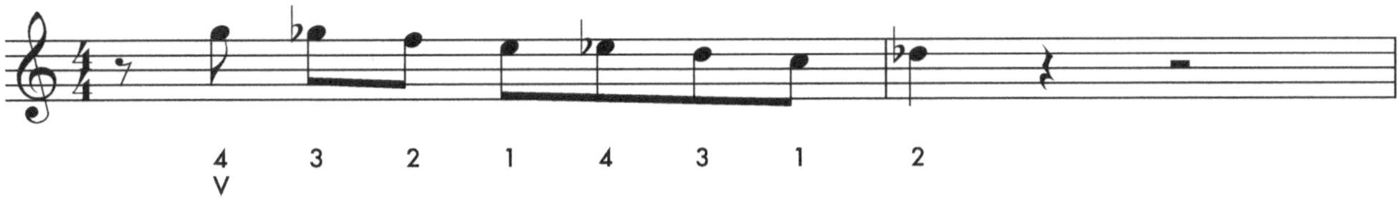

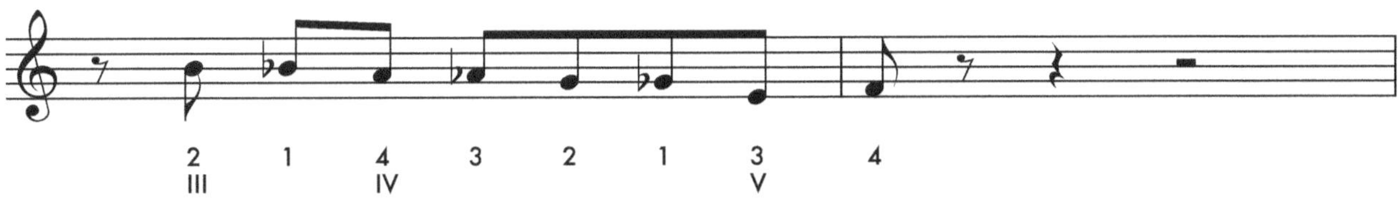

This phrase includes a chromatic figure that is associated with Miles Davis. There are multiple ways of viewing this device. It could be perceived as a series of chromatic enclosures descending in half steps, each folding into the next, providing endless potential points of departure to connect to other ideas. Where the sequence starts rhythmically will have a crucial impact on how it is perceived.

Experiment with expanding or contracting the device and connecting to different ideas ascending or descending out of the pattern. Here are some examples that extend the device to create other points of departure. These examples are only a starting point meant to illustrate the process of exploration.

3 4 2 3 1 2 1 1 3 4 2 3
VI V VI
3 4 2 3 1 2 1 1 3 4 2 3 1 2
VI V VI
3 4 2 3 1 2 1 1 3 4 2 3 1 2 1 1
VI V VI V VI
3 4 2 3 1 2 1 1 3 4 2 3 1 2 1 1 3 4
VI V VI V VI VII
3 4 2 3 1 2 1 1 3 4 2 3 1 2 1 1 3 4 2 3
VI V VI V VI VII

Line 6

♩ = 214

Source: G Minor Blues

Line 6 Notes

The first phrase of this line is built off of cells using fourths and fifths.

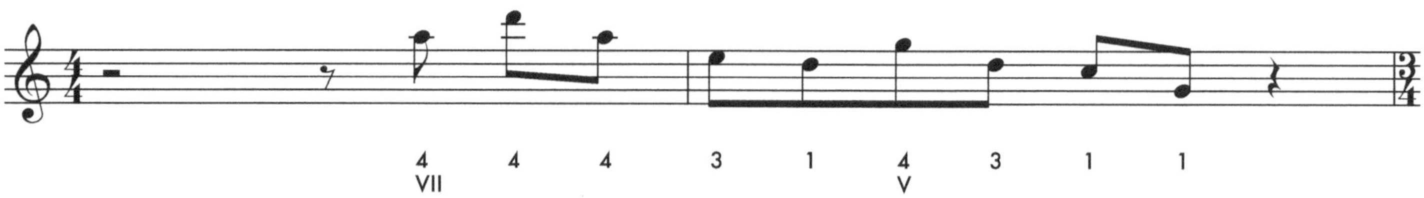

The phrase utilizes three pitch formations that are effectively different inversions or rotations of the same shape. These shapes are used throughout the lines in this book in both basic and expanded forms. Miles Okazaki's "351 Shapes" book, available online as a PDF, is a valuable reference for pitch shapes. This is Shape 65 in the Okazaki book.

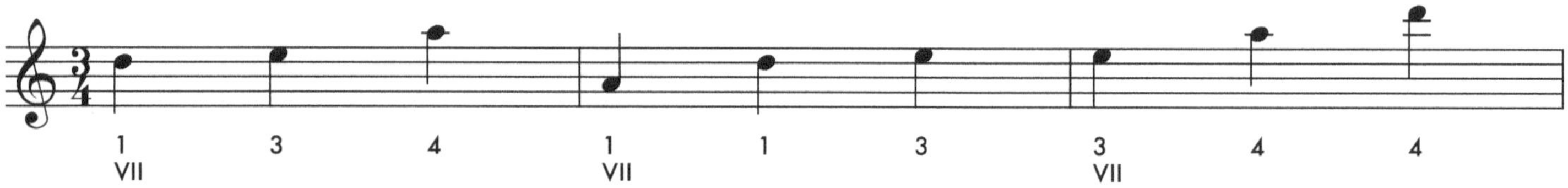

Expanding and contracting these shapes in different ways creates many melodic and rhythmic possibilities and the potential to cover a wide range of the instrument. The cells are moveable devices that can be transposed and combined to work in many harmonic contexts. Practice the shapes throughout the range of the instrument and experiment with different fingerings.

As an exploratory exercise, try creating a chain of cells that each begin a half step above or below the last note of the previous cell. Here is an example using this concept.

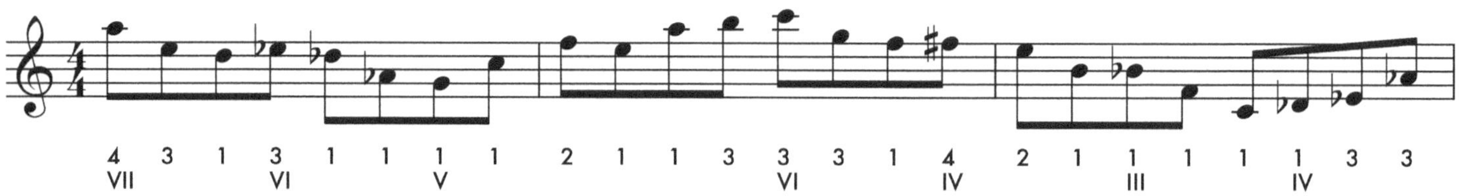

This phrase creates a sequence of major triads descending in whole tones.

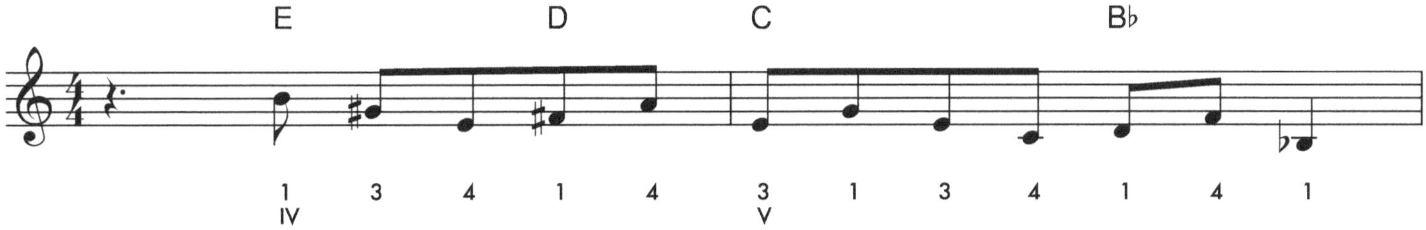

Notice that the triad pairs are played in two different forms. The first two triads, E major and D major, are played as a contracted form of the figure below, with one note removed from the beginning and end of the shape.

As an exercise, extend the idea to include another triad pair, a major third above E, to create a complete chain of major triads played in whole tones. Practicing the seven-note figure as continuous eighth notes, its relationship with the beat shifts between upbeats and downbeats. Play the exercise in other subdivisions (triplets, sixteenths, quintuplets, etc.) and notice how it shifts through the beat in various ways.

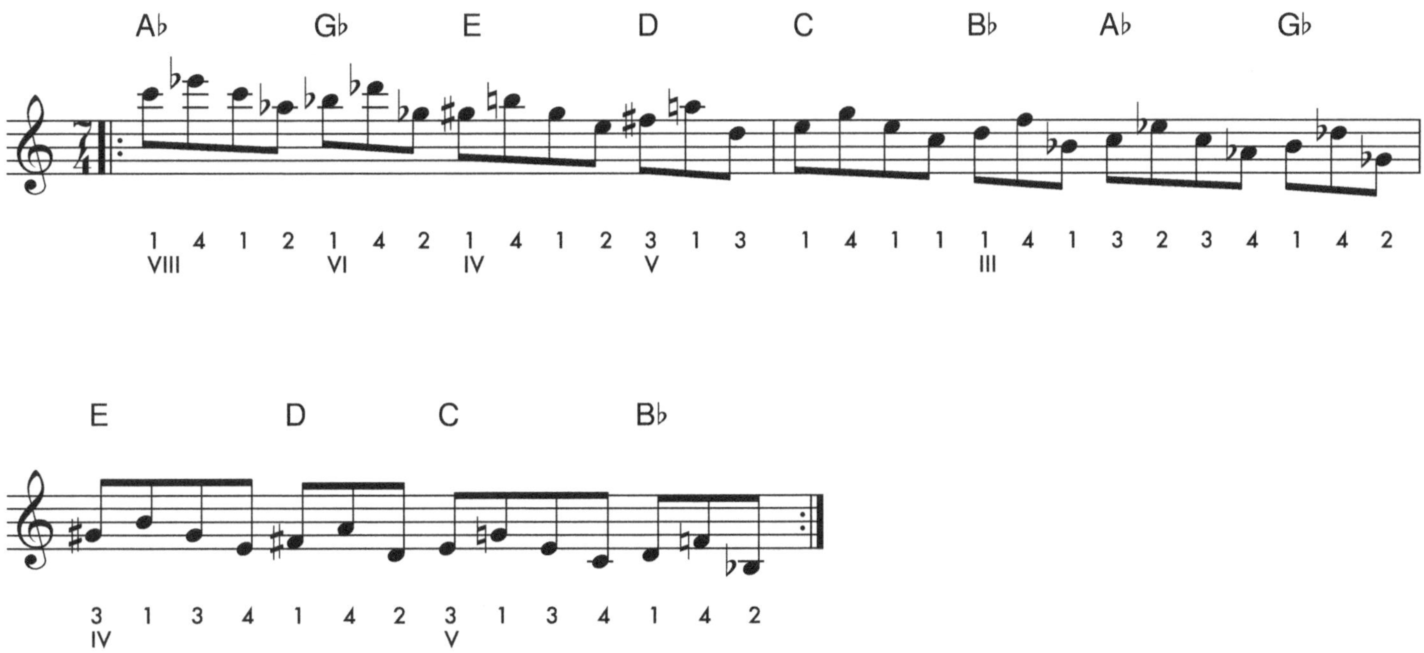

Line 7

♩ = 87 Source: Darn That Dream

Line 7 Notes

Here are the first two figures of this line, a seven-note figure and a five-note figure, notated as quarter notes.

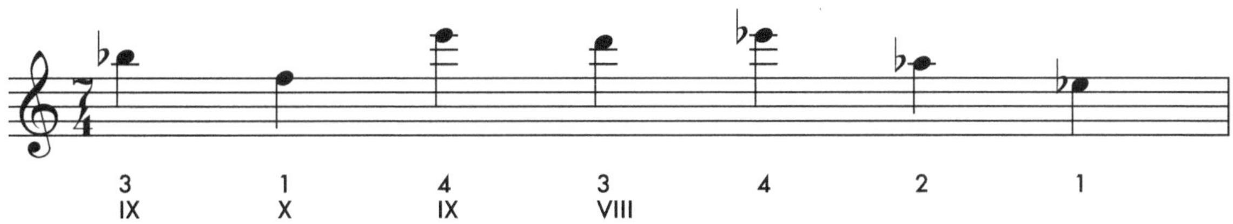

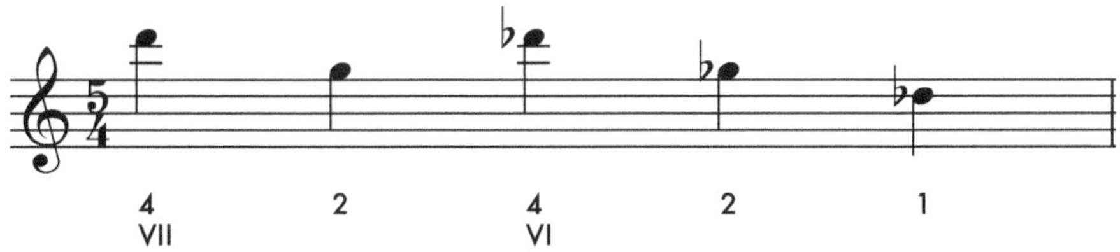

As an exercise, practice each figure in different rhythmic subdivisions, as notated in the examples below. In addition, practice playing the shapes more loosely and lyrically. The application of this type of figure does not always call for an exacting rhythmic interpretation but for the effect of speeding up or slowing down or the gestures created by different note groupings.

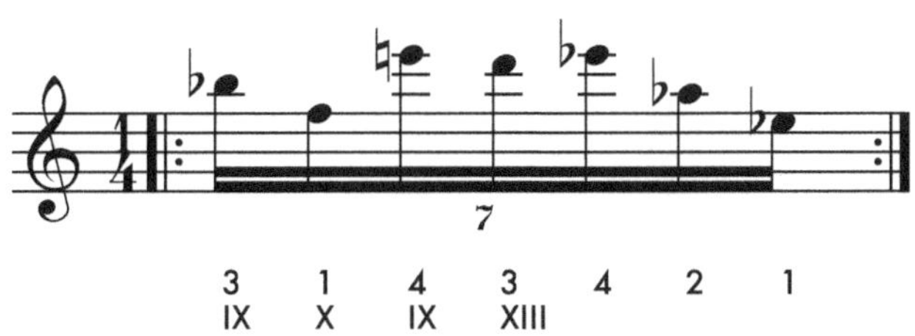

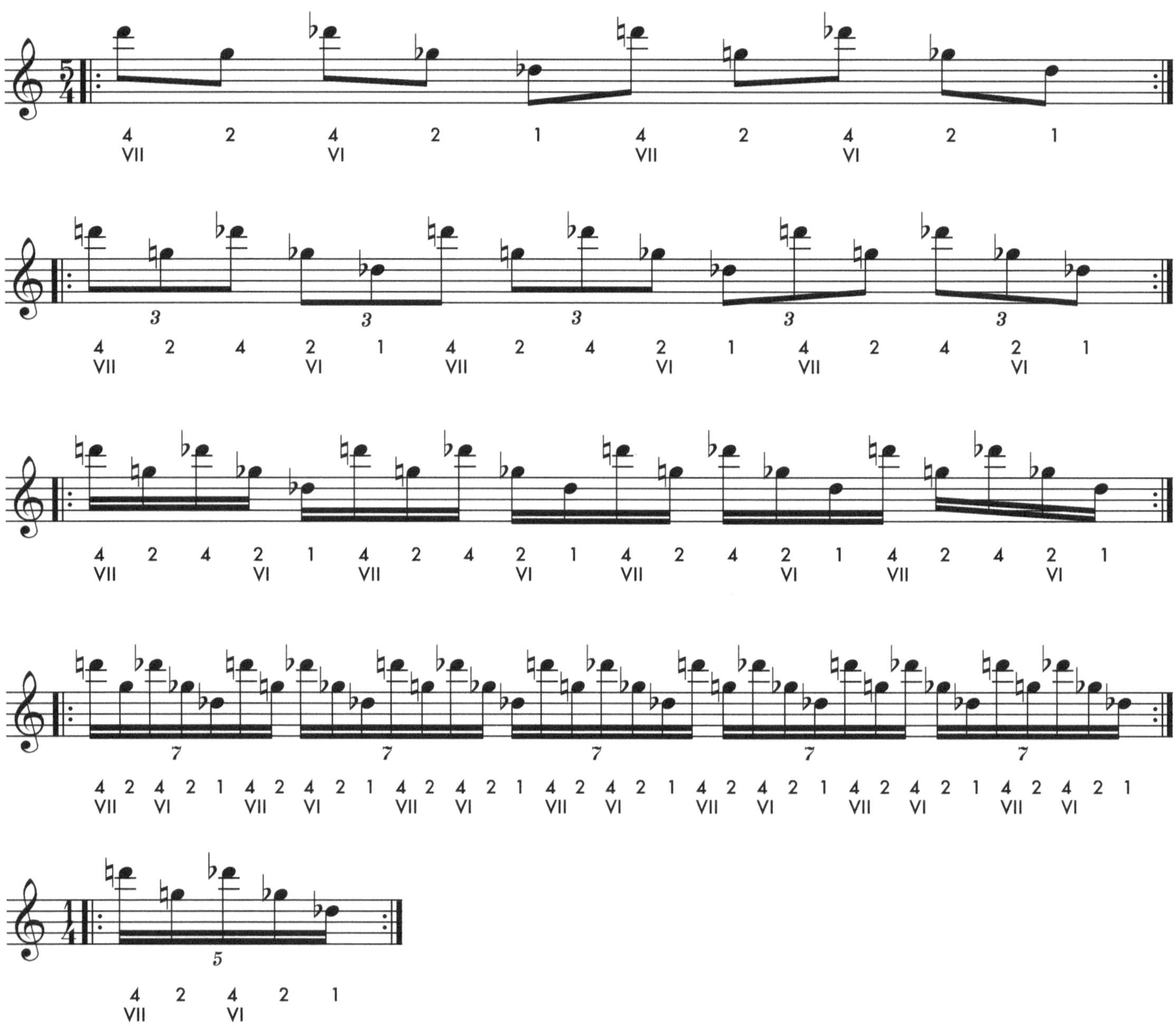

Practice combining the figures and moving them around in different intervals. Here is an example exercise looking at one possible way of applying this concept.

Another technique employed in this line is legato chromatics, played by sliding on a single finger or using hammer-ons or pull-offs.

Here is an example exercise to work on legato chromatics. Try playing this with a variety of techniques, including using any single finger or combination of fingers, sliding, or using hammer-ons and pull-offs. The notated fingerings are a guide for some of the possibilities. As you work on the lines presented in this book, consider the mechanical skills required and the issues you have in your playing and devise exercises to get the sound you seek.

Line 8

♩ = 70 Source: A Minor Vamp

Line 8 Notes

This line alternates between chromatic phrases and arpeggios or scalar fragments. The chromatic phrases are consistently descending, while the arpeggios and scalar phrases alternate between ascending and descending figures.

Work on alternating between chromatics, arpeggios, and scalar fragments as an exercise. Each of these fundamental musical elements can be studied in isolation. However, by consciously connecting or alternating between them, you must make quick adjustments and maintain a sense of musical balance, developing your control over each element.

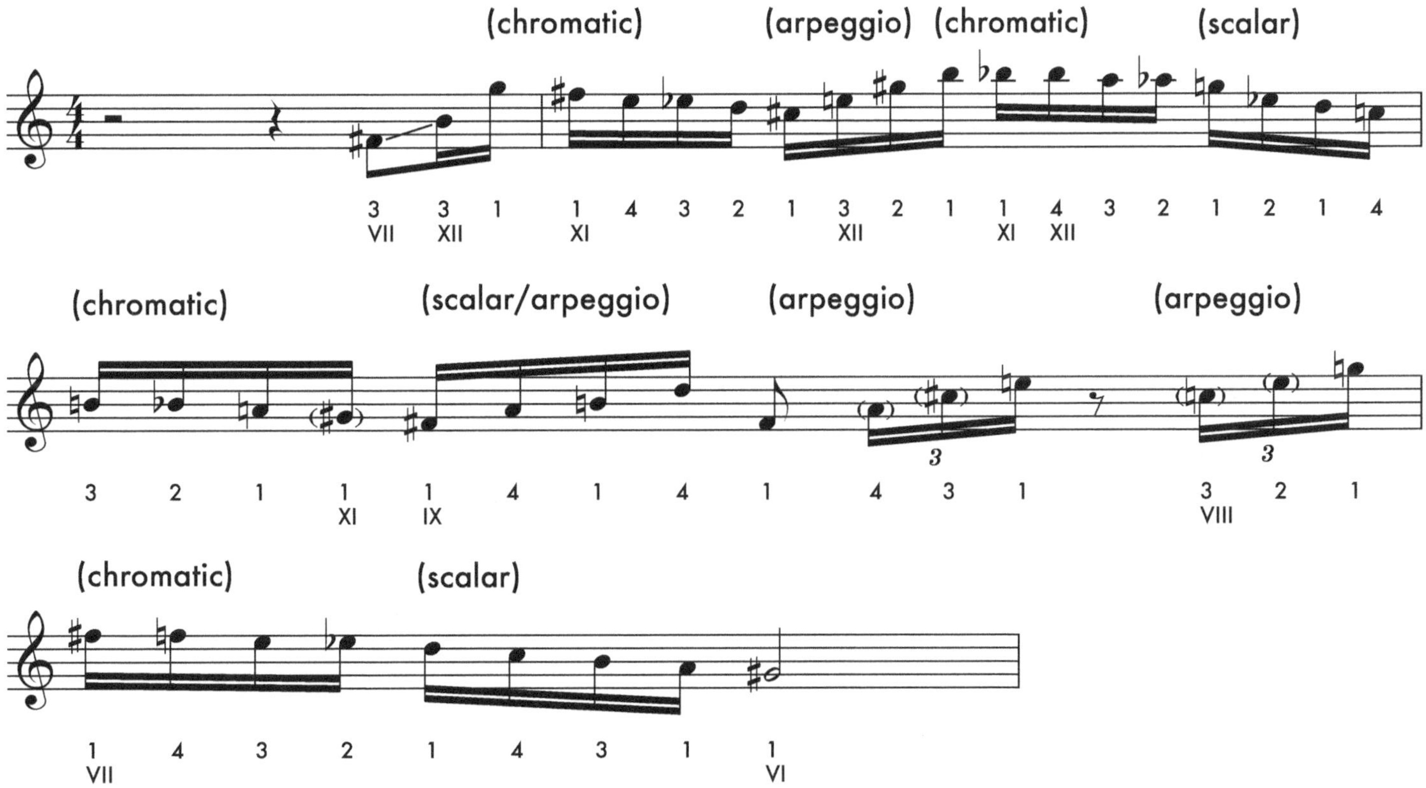

Although this line is played on an A minor vamp, many of the phrases include cadences targeting the V chord, E7. Introducing phrases built off of or targeting the dominant of the tonality can help create a sense of tension and release when playing on a static harmony. With this in mind, experiment using devices and lines you already know to build tension by resolving to or targeting the V chord of the tonality you are playing in.

Line 9

♩ = 228 **Source: Blues in F**

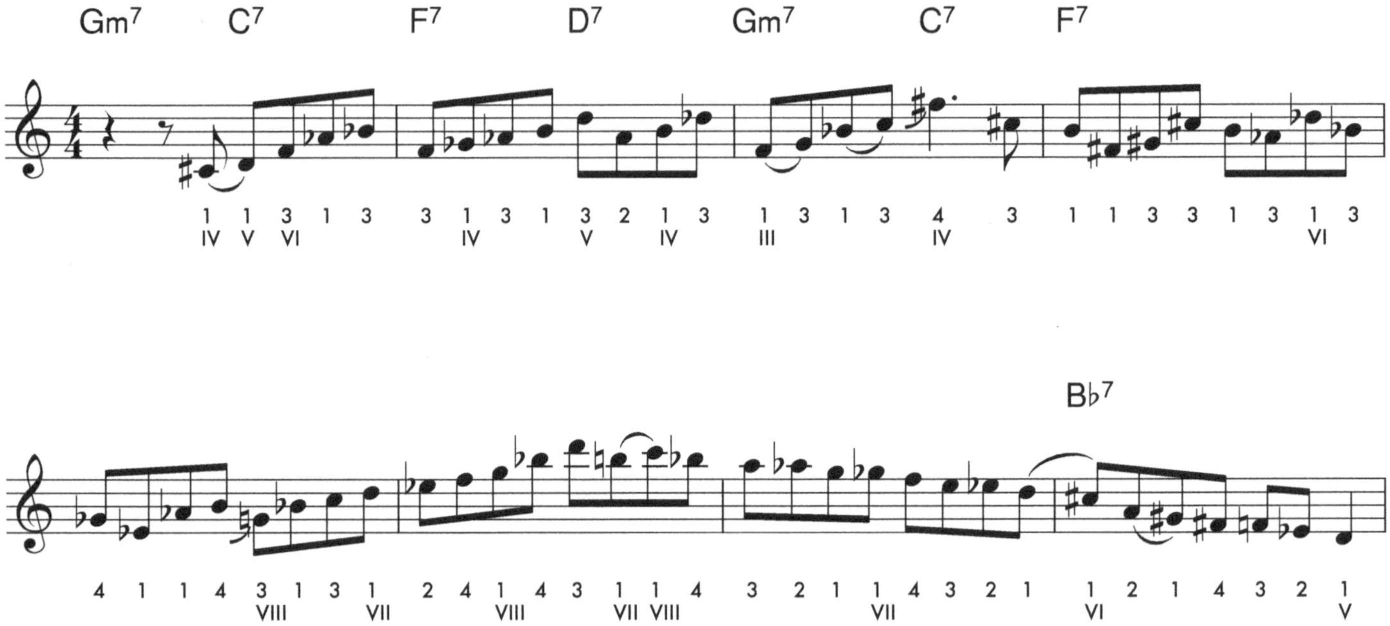

Line 9 Notes

Notice how this phrase is played using only the first and third fingers, covering a variety of intervals by using slides, shifts, and leaps.

Consider which melodic shapes would be generated by using the same fingering without shifting. You will recognize this as a standard fingering for the minor pentatonic scale.

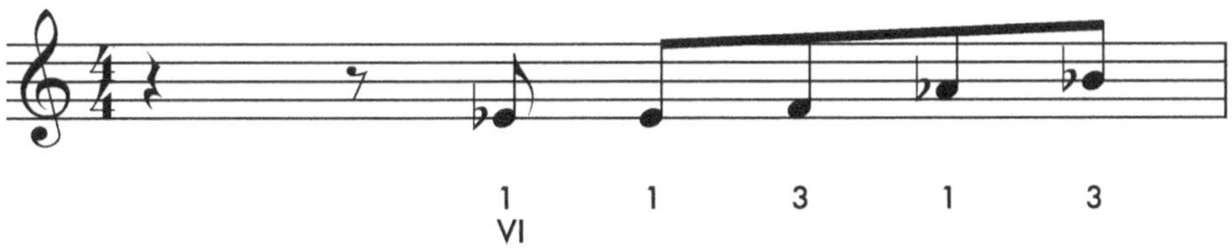

To take advantage of the natural strength of the hand while also exploring a multitude of melodic possibilities, try using familiar fingerings and shifting positions to get different intervallic combinations necessary for various musical ideas.

Here is an example exercise to explore potential note combinations using the fingering for the figure above, retaining the same starting note (F) and number of notes in the melodic shape (5).

1 3 3 1 3 1 3 3 1 3 1 3 3 1 3 1 3 3 1 3 1 3 3 1
IV VI IV VI III IV VI III VI V III VI IV

3 1 3 3 1 3 1 3
III VI III

Line 10

♩ = 214

Source: G Minor Blues

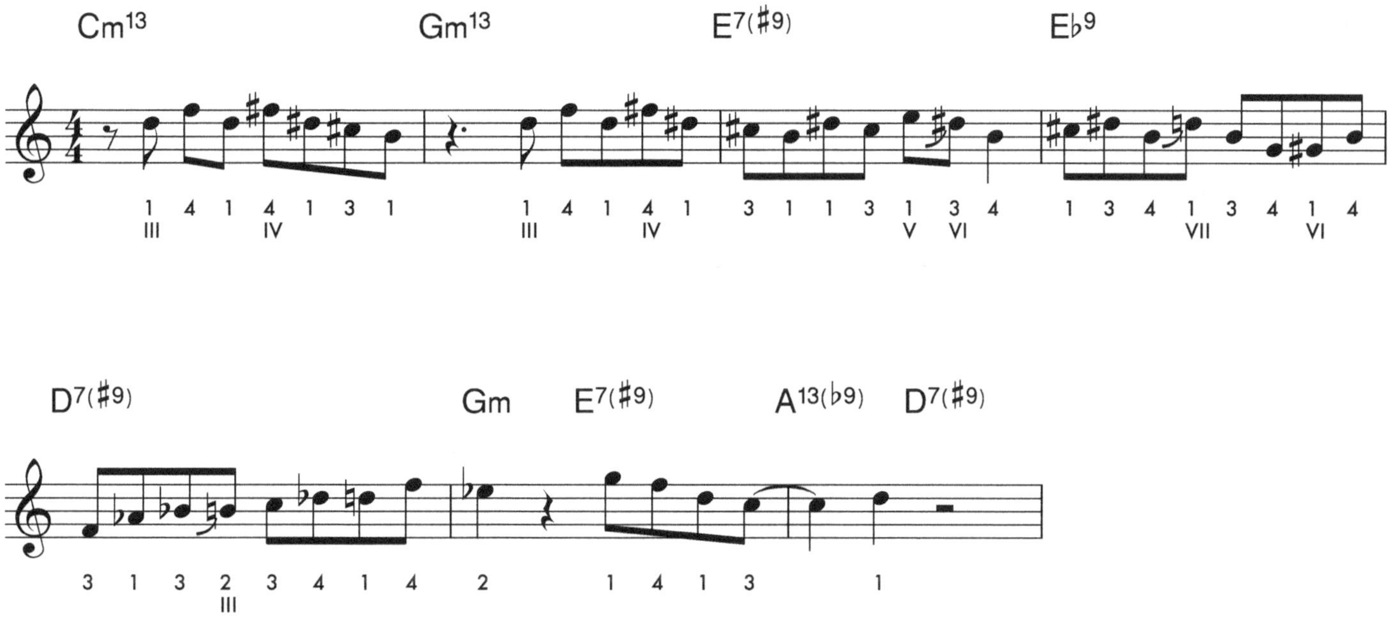

Line 10 Notes

This phrase includes two figures that shift upward on the guitar mid-idea and ends with a figure that shifts downward on the guitar mid-idea.

Notice that without the shifts, the fingerings used correspond to familiar shapes, often found in scale patterns played in a single position.

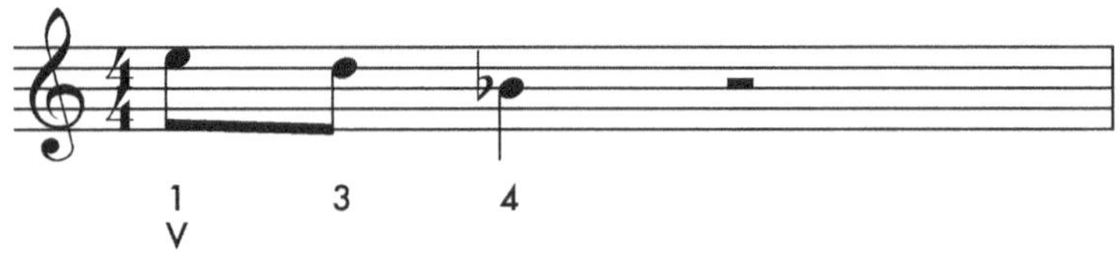

Explore how these physical shapes can generate a range of melodic figures by shifting at various points in the shape. A shape that is moved around in its entirety can be recognized as a transposition of that shape. By utilizing the physical framework of complete cells while shifting in different places, it is possible to generate the impression of a shape and the natural phrasing that comes with it without repeating the exact melodic figures.

Here are some examples implementing this approach. Observe how this technique is used throughout the lines in this book, and explore the possibilities by shifting shapes and phrases that you already know.

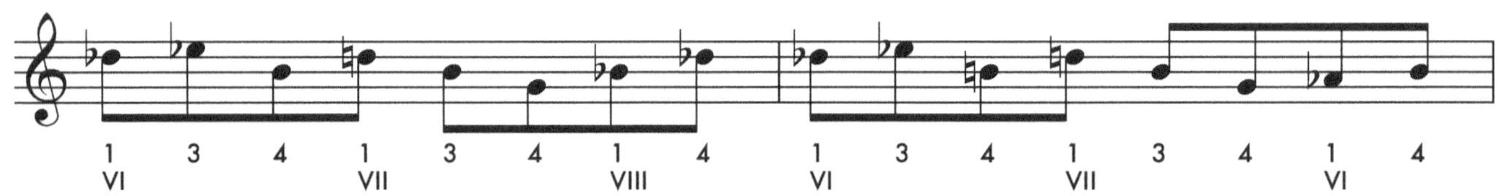

A critical feature of this line is how the phrase length changes, beginning with a short idea, then expanding, and finally contracting for the closing statement. As a result, it sounds and feels conversational. Be mindful of phrasing patterns in your day-to-day conversations and interactions, and consider how you could apply these structures in your musical statements.

Line 11

♩ = 252 Source: Impressions

Line 11 Notes

This phrase is built with arpeggios organized into four and five-note groupings. The groupings are clearly marked by the starting note of an ascending arpeggio.

Continuing this idea through the scale generates an exercise to develop our understanding of arpeggios and a rhythmic device that utilizes nine notes in groupings of four and five. Playing three or four-note arpeggios is more common, so playing a five-note arpeggio is also good training to gain familiarity with the "upper structures" of chords.

Practice the exercise above in different subdivisions. Note that in duple subdivisions, the figure will flip between downbeats and upbeats. Here is an example of a partial version of the exercise in 9/8, feeling the beat in three.

While this line is played in the context of the D minor tonality, there are some significant departures. This section of the line veers from D minor into E♭ minor and back, woven together using fourths and chromatic language.

There are many possible ways of analyzing this type of movement. Instead of focusing on the theoretical aspects of it, one effective way of working on incorporating these sounds is to use a drone, backing track, or looping pedal to create a static harmonic environment. With this context, work on playing lines in any tonality other than the primary harmonic environment. Move between the home tonality and other tonalities, exploring the different spaces that each respective tonality introduces. This practice is excellent training for your ear and heart to accept and find joy in sounds outside of the musical expectations you may have developed.

With many of the lines in this book, the magic is in how smaller cells and phrases are combined into more complex, extended ideas. The definition of a cell or phrase is personal and dynamic depending on the context, so there is generally more than one way to perceive the breakdown of cells within a line or phrase. In studying the lines, one helpful practice is to isolate what you identify as a discreet cell, phrase, or statement. While this process is not always clear-cut, there is great benefit in identifying these cells. Training your mind to comprehend melodic and rhythmic ideas as units will significantly impact how you hear and perceive music and your ability to spontaneously combine and reframe musical material.

On the following page, see an example of one way of identifying and isolating cells and phrases from Line 11:

2 4 1 2 4 1 4
IV
2 4 1 4
2 1 1 3 1 2 1
III V
4 1 1
3 1 2 1 3 4 1 3
VII
2 1 4 4 1 2 1 4
4 2 1 4 1 4 3 1 4
2 2 2 1 2 1 4 3 2 1 2 1 4
VIII
1 3 4 1 1 3 4 1 1
VI V

Line 12

♩ = 51

Source: It Could Happen To You

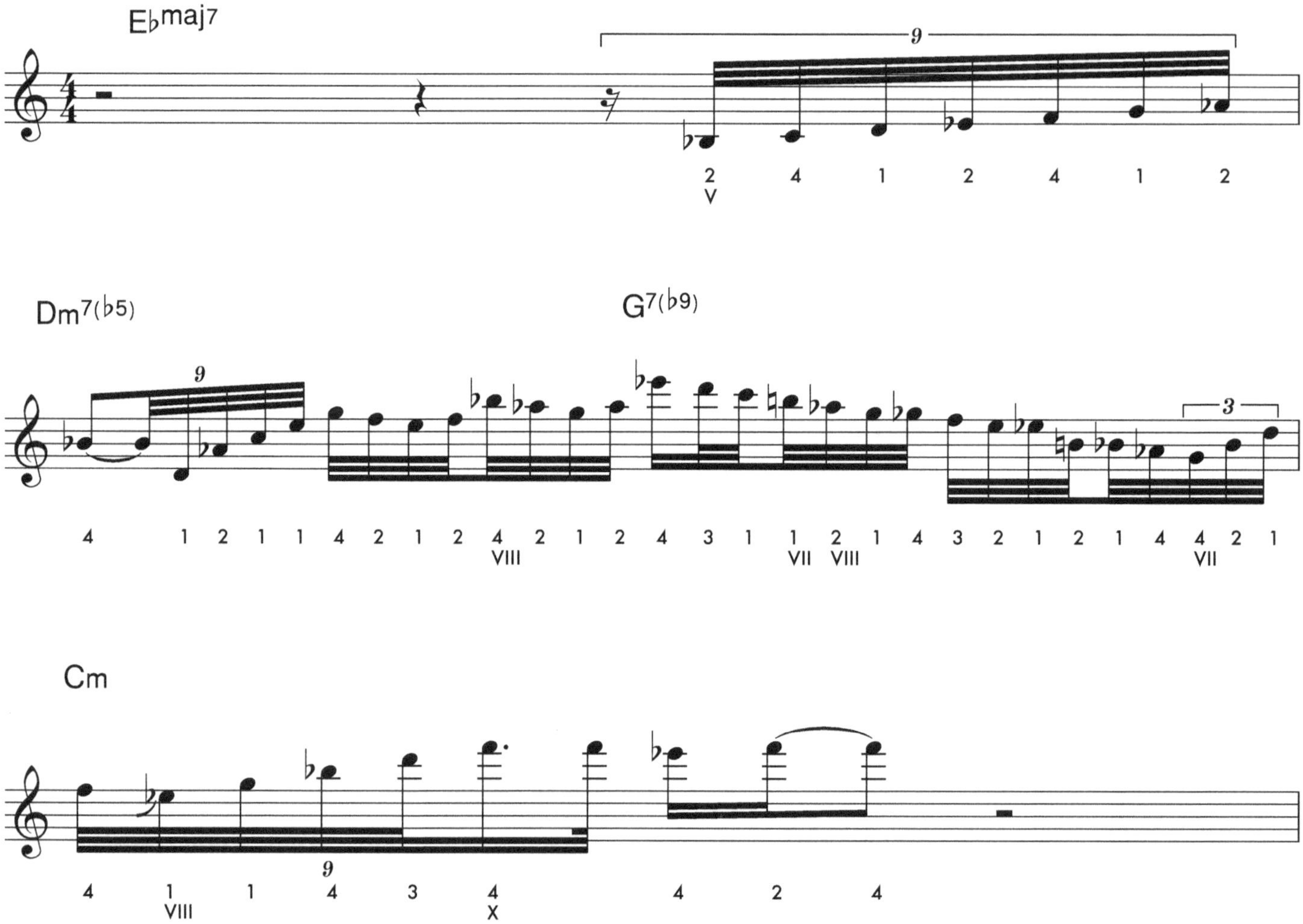

Line 12 Notes

Notice that this phrase is generated by a chord voicing for Dm7♭5 with the natural ninth, moving the top note from the ninth to the eleventh to the third to derive a melodic line. Using chord voicings as physical frames can provide stable, moveable figures to generate single-note lines. The intervallic structure of chord voicings, and the way the chord tones are distributed in different types of voicings, can lead to many fresh melodic possibilities using familiar physical shapes.

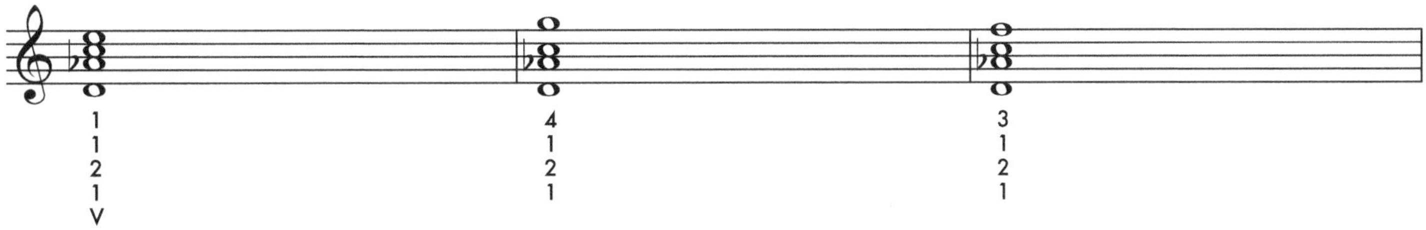

Here is a ii-V-i idea derived by moving this chord shape up a minor third. First, memorize the basic idea and practice it in all the keys. Then, practice creating variations and extending them to connect to other melodic phrases.

This melodic idea, built off of two arpeggios, G-7 and E♭maj7, is applied here on a C minor chord. Consider how the same idea could be applied on different chords and the harmonic implications and colors that emerge when using it in other contexts.

Some suggestions: E♭ major, A♭ major, F minor, A-7♭5, Fsus, B♭13, G7

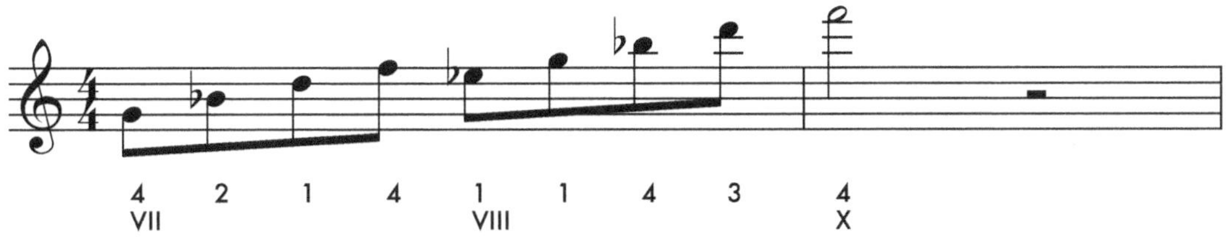

Line 13

♩ = 158

Source: Jeannine

Line 13 Notes

This line begins with a minor seventh arpeggio played with a fingering built from a repeated shape using only fingers one and four, shifting up by two frets and highlighting a structural characteristic of the minor seventh chord.

The minor seventh chord (or major sixth chord) is comprised of two sets of minor thirds a fifth apart **or**, inverted, two sets of major sixths a fifth apart.

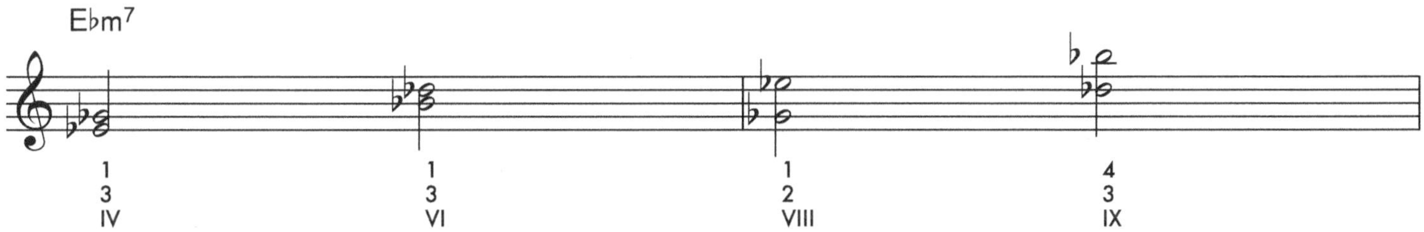

Continuing this line of thinking, notice that combining two sets of major thirds a fifth apart, **or** inverted as minor sixths a fifth apart, generates in a major seventh chord.

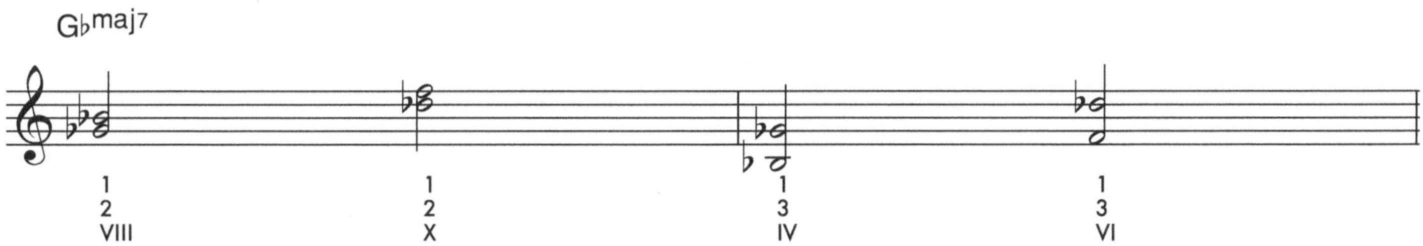

These realizations can lead to fresh ways of exploring and furthering your fretboard knowledge. Here are two example exercises using minor thirds a fifth apart for E♭m7 and major thirds a fifth apart for G♭maj7.

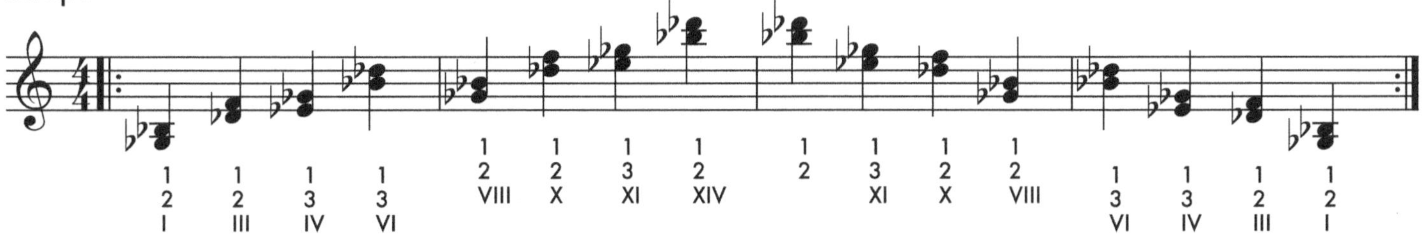

Line 14

♩ = 113 Source: Lover Man

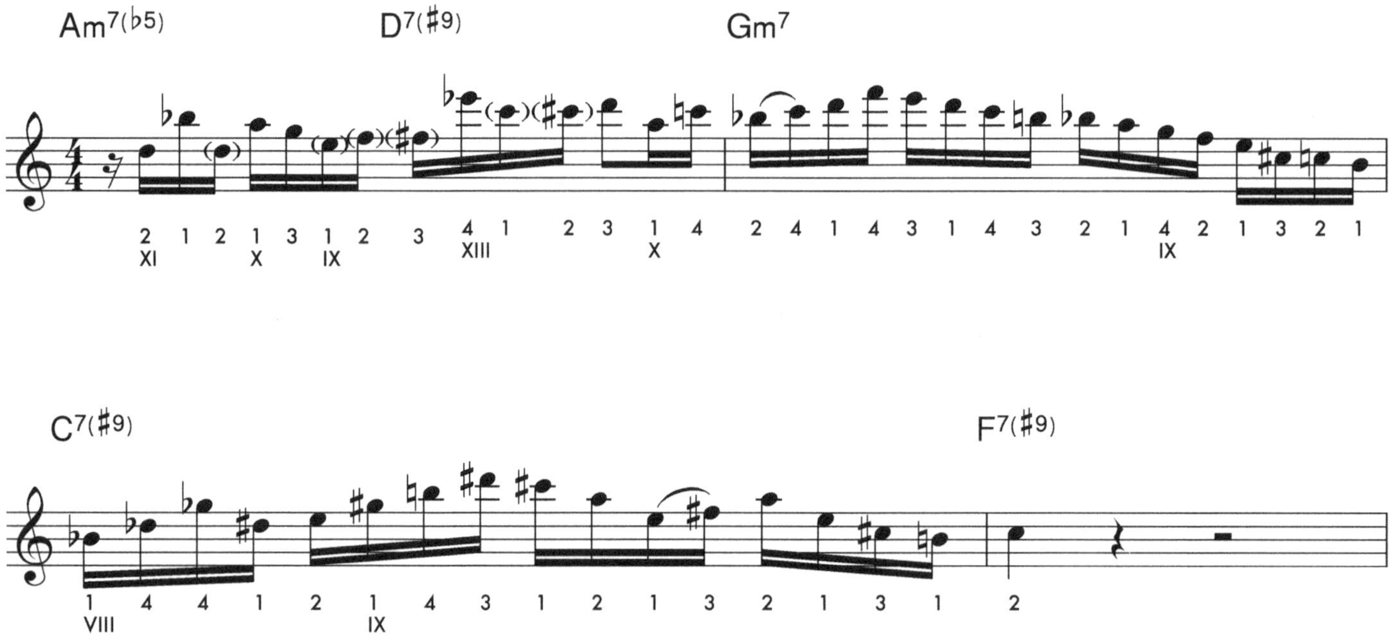

Line 14 Notes

This phrase uses chromatic approach notes and enclosures, a core part of the language developed by Charlie Parker, Dizzy Gillespie, Thelonious Monk, and others. Devices and phrases from the lexicon of musical ideas that these musicians innovated and passed on to others in their sphere are the basis of much of the language of creative music today.

Notably, in Line 14 the device is more felt than heard. While the notes are fingered on the guitar, some are ghosted.

Here is the same idea notated as an eighth note line. The phrase targets the third and root of D7, starting a half step above the target notes, descending a minor third, then playing chromatically from a whole step below into the target.

Locate various potential fingerings to play this phrase, and practice playing it through all 12 keys and in different subdivisions. This work will help you see and hear chord tones and the chromatic pitches surrounding them throughout the instrument.

Here is one idea for extending this phrase to target the fifth of the chord as well.

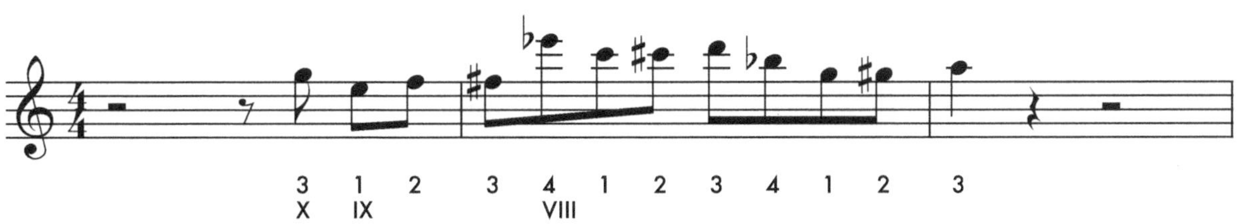

Here is an example exercise using the device, targeting the third, root, and fifth, played through the circle of fourths in a triplet feel. This is a beneficial mental and physical exercise to increase awareness of chord tones and surrounding chromatics of major triads through all keys. First, try this as written to get a sense of the movements, then work on playing through the keys using this general phrase as a point of departure for your lines. Once comfortable moving the phrase through fourths, try other movements (whole tones, semitones, minor thirds, major thirds, etc.).

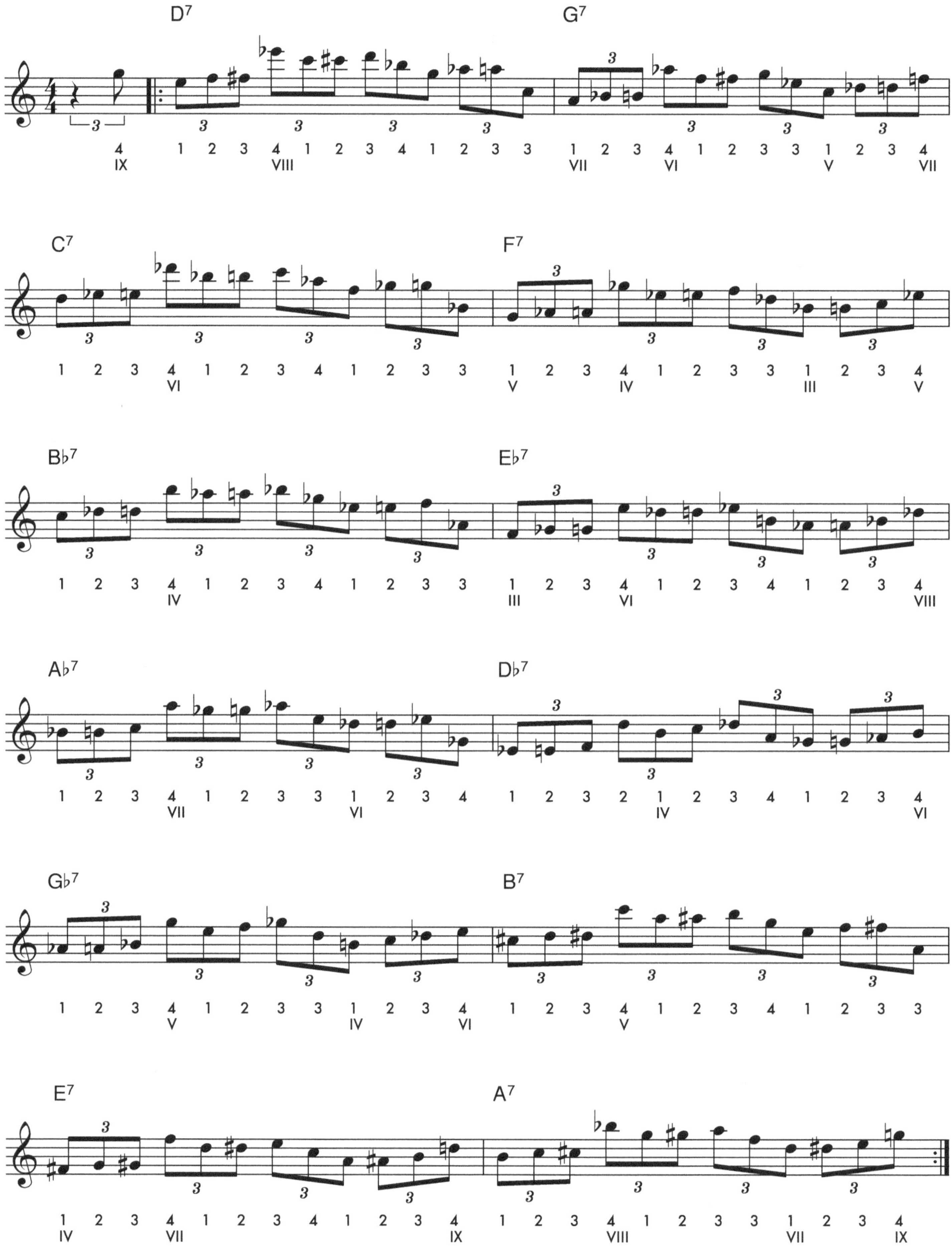
D7 G7
4 1 2 3 4 1 2 3 4 1 2 3 3 1 2 3 4 1 2 3 3 1 2 3 4
IX VIII VII VI V VII
C7 F7
1 2 3 4 1 2 3 4 1 2 3 3 1 2 3 4 1 2 3 3 1 2 3 4
VI V IV III V
B♭7 E♭7
1 2 3 4 1 2 3 4 1 2 3 3 1 2 3 4 1 2 3 4 1 2 3 4
IV III VI VIII
A♭7 D♭7
1 2 3 4 1 2 3 3 1 2 3 4 1 2 3 2 1 2 3 4 1 2 3 4
VII VI IV VI
G♭7 B7
1 2 3 4 1 2 3 3 1 2 3 4 1 2 3 4 1 2 3 4 1 2 3 3
V IV VI V
E7 A7
1 2 3 4 1 2 3 4 1 2 3 4 1 2 3 4 1 2 3 3 1 2 3 4
IV VII IX VIII VII IX

Line 15

♩ = 194

Source: Blues Minor

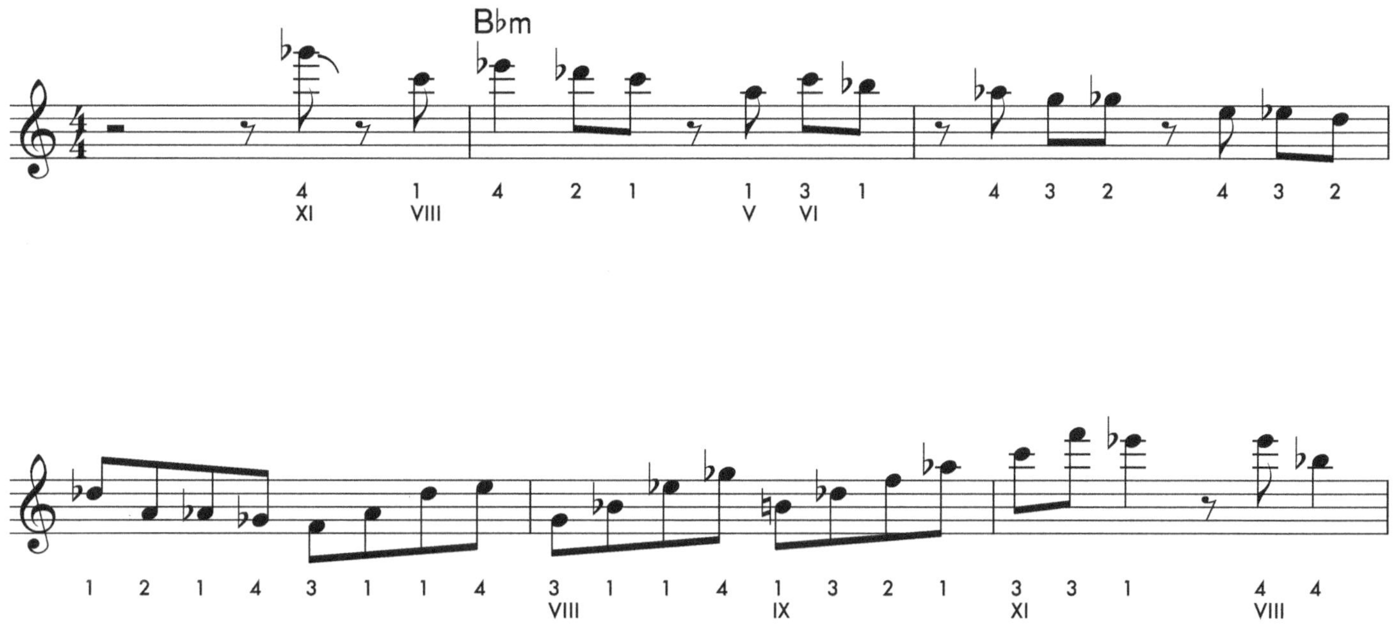

Line 15 Notes

Notice how the same enclosure is used twice in this line, each time on the same string but with a different fingering. Consider why the same melodic shape may be played differently depending on where it is coming from and where it is going. Becoming more aware of the various ways that a melodic idea can be played on the instrument helps to avoid treating any idea as routine and can help to illuminate numerous diverging pathways from a single idea.

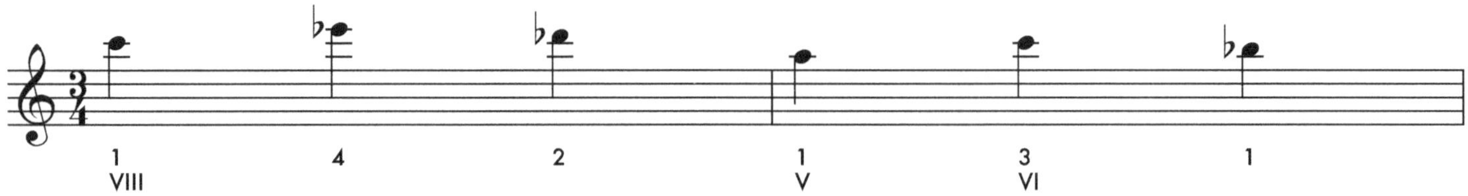

An essential characteristic of this phrase is the rhythmic spacing and where the breaths occur. It is a "broken" chromatic sequence leading into a descending altered dominant phrase.

Notice how you get an unbroken chromatic line from B♭ to D♭ by filling in the rhythmic spaces.

Experiment with breaking up chromatic sequences in various ways to create different rhythmic phrases. The underlying chromatic movement can help create flow. Also, try adding and subtracting notes from chromatic phrases.

This shape is played twice in Line 15. It is easily moveable and draws upon a dual feeling of major and minor. One way of viewing it is as a major ♯9 chord starting on the third.

Notice the symmetry of the shape around the axis of the two middle pitches (A♭/D♭, B♭/E♭). A♭ to F is a minor third down and D♭ to E is a minor third up. B♭ to G is a minor third down and E♭ to G♭ is a minor third up. This generates both a major and minor chord with the lowest note in the figure being the major third and the highest note being the minor third. This shape's symmetry and dual nature allow for flexibility in its application, leaving many possible pathways available.

Line 16

♩ = 120

Source: A Night in Tunisia

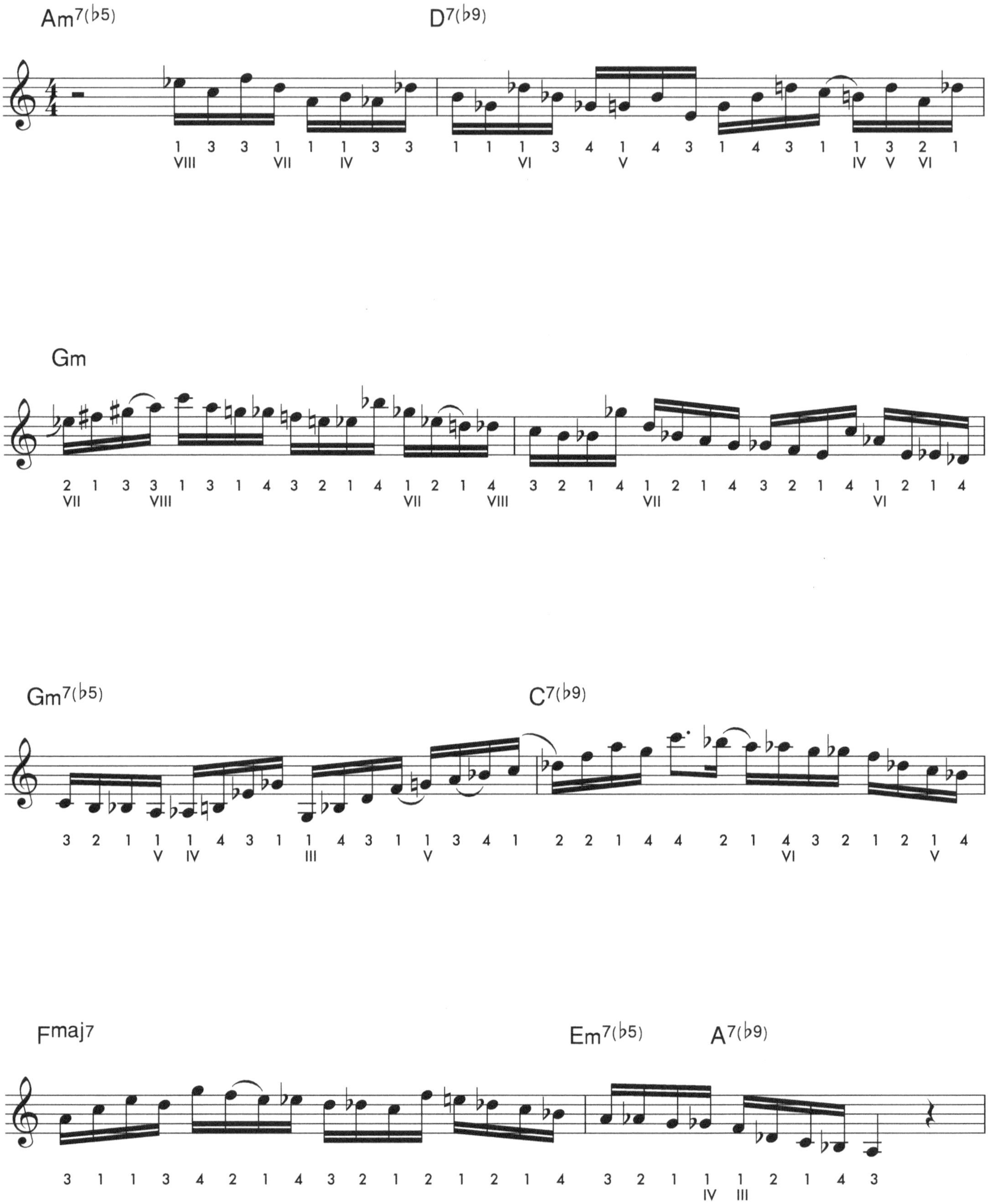

Line 16 Notes

One way of perceiving the first four phrases of this line is as melodic shapes with rhythmic groupings of five, six, and seven. Repeating the phrases (5 + 5 + 6 + 7) with a steady beat generates an exercise for hearing and feeling odd rhythmic phrases. In a rhythmic subdivision of sixteenth notes the total number of notes in the four phrases adds up to twenty-three, one sixteenth note shy of six beats. So as we repeat the cycle it will shift one sixteenth note back each time, landing on the beat again after four repetitions, or twenty-three beats.

Here is the same idea notated in a triplet feel.

This section of the line repeats a device, descending chromatics leading to an ascending interval leap of a fifth or minor sixth.

The same fingering is used for the device on different string sets, yielding a leap of a fifth between the G and B strings and a leap of a minor sixth on other string sets.

Line 17

♩ = 70

Source: Willow Weep For Me

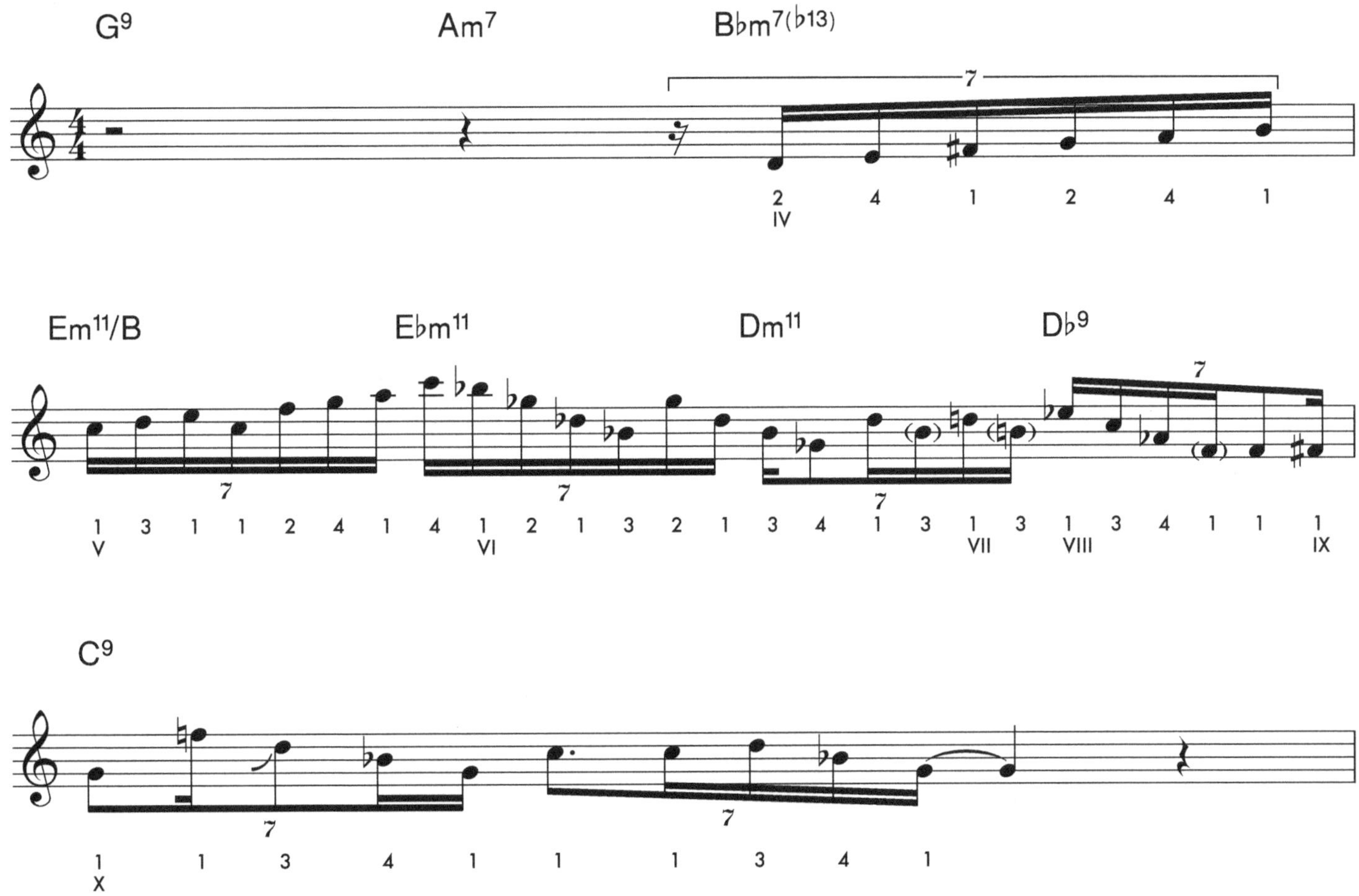

Line 17 Notes

Ghosting notes is a core aspect of the feeling of many of the lines in this book. This line includes an effective device using ghost notes, played here as minor thirds, with the lower note struck by the left hand but not plucked by the right hand. This could be called a hammer-on, but since the lower note is on a different string, you do not get a sustained pitch leading into the next. In this context, the dynamic difference between the lower and higher notes creates a ghosting effect, with the lower note being significantly quieter.

Here are some suggested ways of practicing ghost notes with this figure in mind. These are only a few examples of the possibilities.

Minor thirds moving in half steps, ascending/descending.

Major thirds moving in half steps, ascending/descending.

Major seconds moving in half steps, ascending/descending.

Minor thirds moving in whole steps, ascending/descending.

Minor thirds moving up a whole step, down a half step ascending, down a whole step, up a half step descending.

This line is notated in a subdivision of seven (septuplets). One way of conceiving of and practicing this subdivision is as combinations of short (2) and long (3) rhythmic pulses. There are three possible permutations of a seven-note cycle using only groups of two or three.

short, short, long (2, 2, 3)
short, long, short (2, 3, 2)
long, short, short (3, 2, 2)

Practice clapping these three patterns with the beat subdivided into septuplets, sixteenths, triplets, and eighths. This will provide some foundation for feeling seven-note figures or subdivisions.

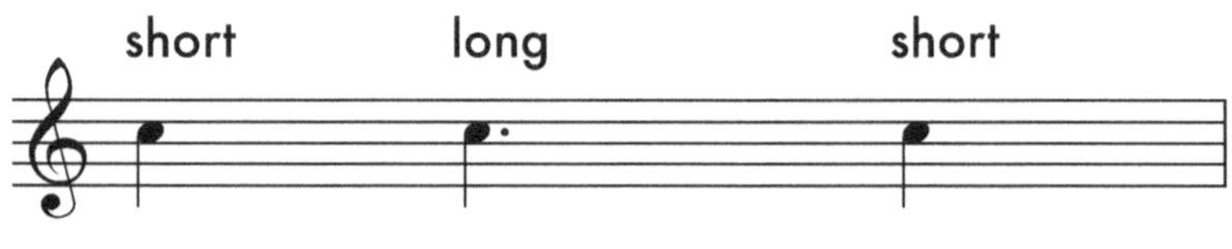

Here is an exercise using a phrase from Line 17, reordering sections of the phrase to practice the various note groupings shown above.

Line 18

♩ = 138

Source: Giant Steps

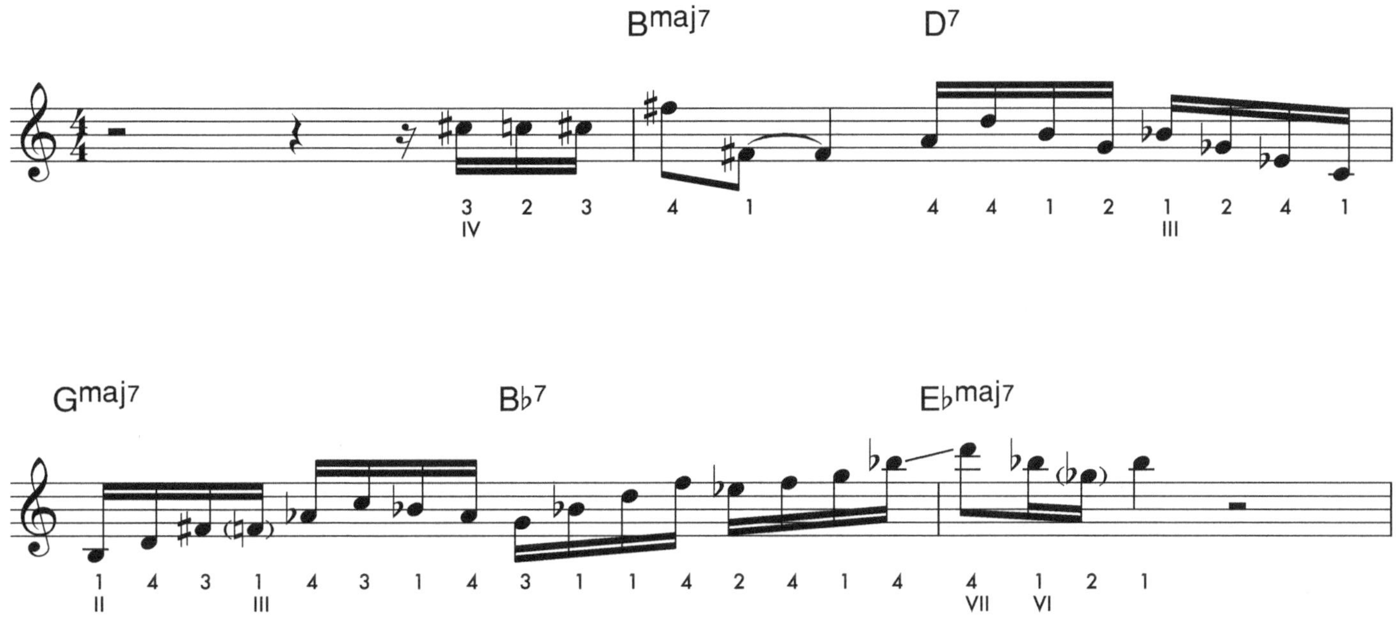

Line 18 Notes

One strategy for processing the devices you discover in the lines in this book (or any material you are studying) is to identify cells that could be applied in different harmonic contexts and move them through a given set of changes. A "cell" that you isolate for study could be a set of pitches alone or a set of pitches associated with a specific rhythm.

Line 18 is played on the first three bars of Giant Steps. So, isolating the first phrase and moving it through the changes of Giant Steps is a great first look at this concept. Keep in mind there are often multiple ways of applying a cell or device to a given chord.

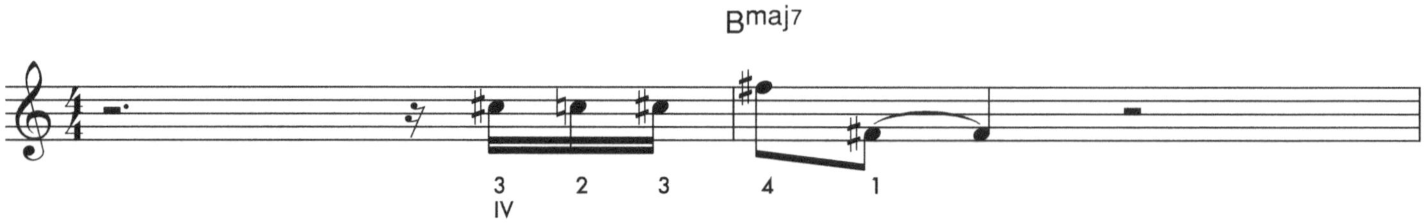

Here is an example of how the device could be applied through the changes. Try developing alternative applications of the same cell, transposing it in different ways through the same set of changes. Also, beyond theoretically thinking through the potential options, put on a backing track and try moving the device around, allowing your ear to dictate whether it sounds "good" or "right" to you. More or less rhythmic space could be used, and the device could also be applied in partial or expanded form.

Many of the phrases in this line could be transposed and applied through the changes. The second phrase includes this idea, resolving D7 to Gmaj7. Phrases that are cadential, dominant to tonic movement, are a great source of material to practice through chord changes and keys.

Applying phrases you have learned through a tune like Giant Steps is a beneficial practice to develop a greater ability to hear and apply various movements. However, as soon as the approach of transposing the same material to different keys is in your ear and under your fingers, practice creating melodic and rhythmic variations. Spending too much time in the world of patterns can create a heaviness and predictability that defies the spirit of the music.

Here is an example of how to apply the V-I phrase from above through the changes of Giant Steps.

E♭maj7 Am7 D7
1 III
4 4 1 2 1 2 4 1
IV III
Gmaj7 C♯m7 F♯7
1 II
4 4 1 2 1 2 4 1
VIII VII
Bmaj7 Fm7 B♭7
1 VI
3 4 1 1 1 1 3 1
VIII VII VI
E♭maj7 C♯m7 F♯7
1 V
4 4 1 2 1 2 4 1
VIII VII

Line 19

♩ = 110

Source: Days of Wine and Roses

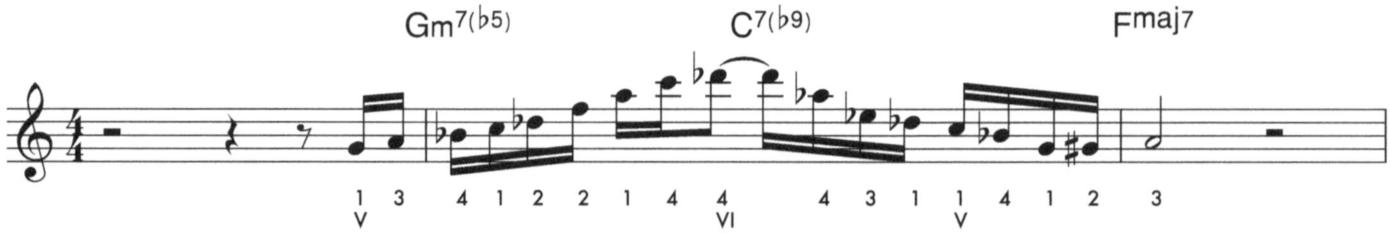

Line 19 Notes

This phrase combines core bebop language with a descending fourths idea in a distinctive way.

As an exercise, create loops of varying lengths using sections of the phrase and observe how the device can be situated rhythmically in different ways. Here are some examples to illustrate this concept. Try these examples, create other loops and variations, and practice connecting the figures to other phrases in your improvisations.

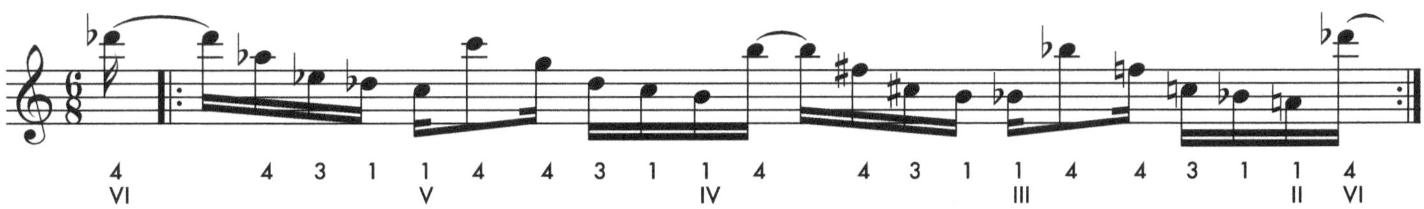

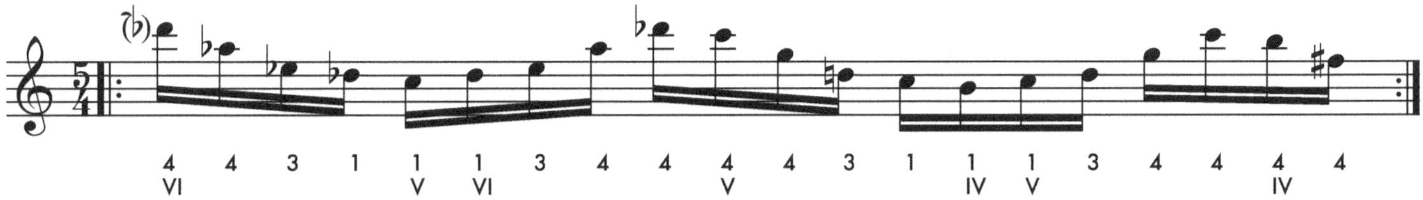

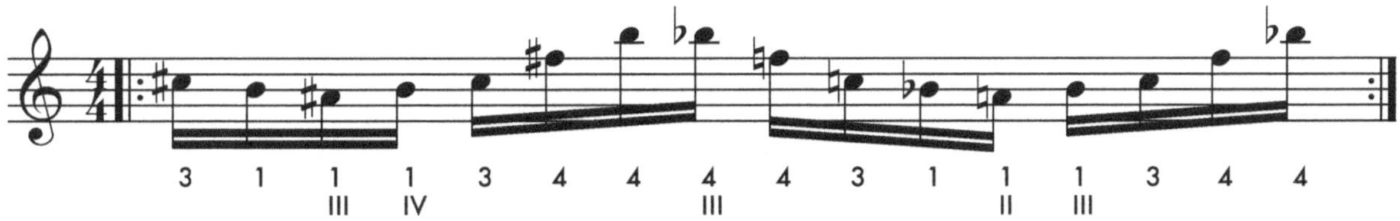

4 4 3 2 1 1 3 4 4 4 4 3 2 1 1 3 4 4
VI V VI V IV
4 4 3 2 1 1 3 4 4 4 4 3 2 1 1 3 4 4
IV III IV III II III

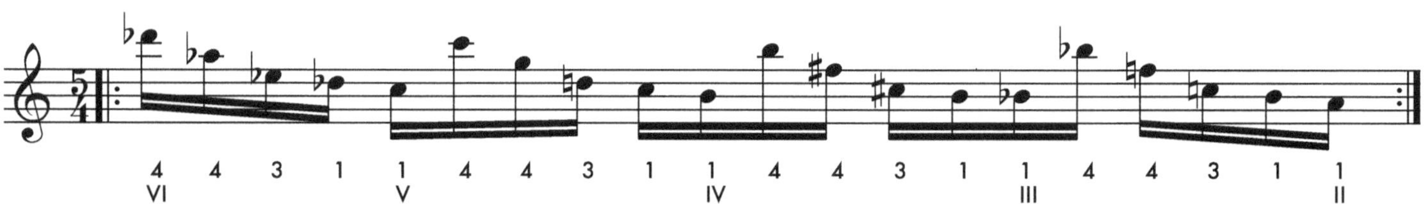
4 4 3 1 1 4 4 3 1 1 4 4 3 1 1 4 4 3 1 1
VI V IV III II

Line 20

♩ = 138

Source: Giant Steps

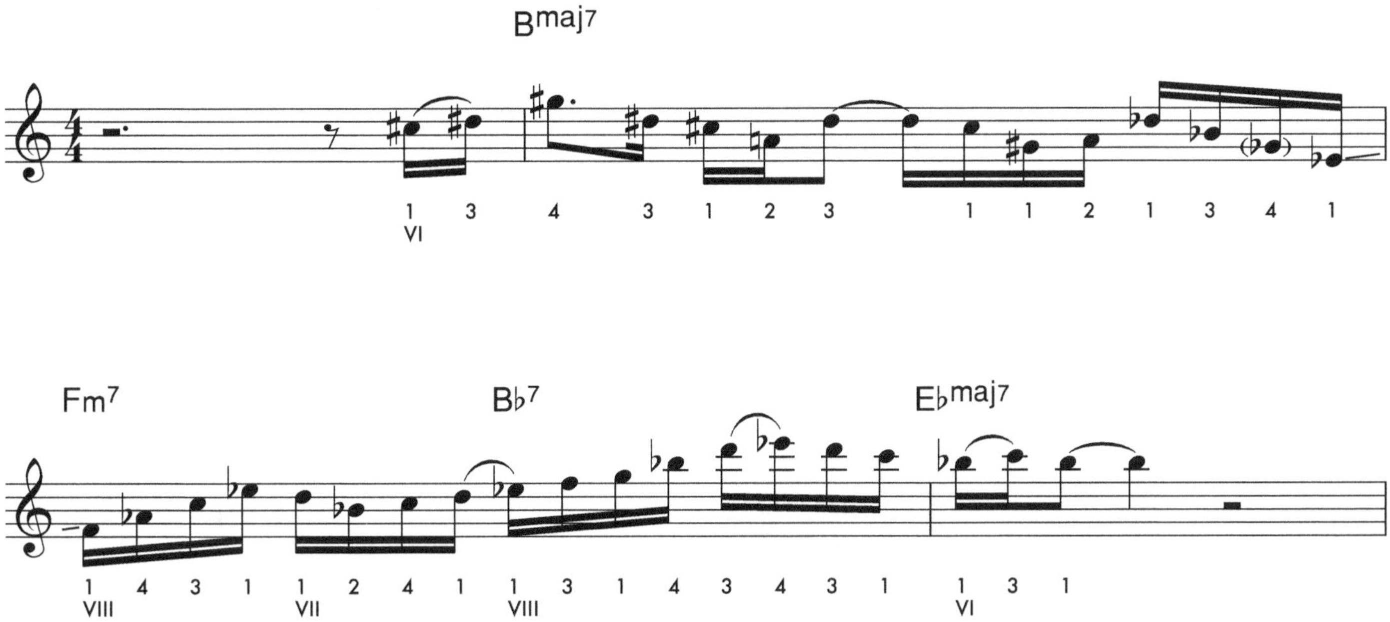

Line 20 Notes

The phrases in this line build from short rhythmic ideas into a longer eighth note statement. The first three phrases form a conversational-sounding rhythmic sentence. It can be perceived as an additive series, starting with three notes, then four notes, then seven notes.

One way to further examine this idea is to isolate the rhythms and practice using the rhythmic content independent from the original pitches. Practice creating melodic statements using this rhythmic framework through the blues and other tunes. Practice with a metronome or drum backing track. Practice leaving different amounts of space between repetitions or using partial or expanded iterations of the idea. Practice connecting this rhythmic sentence with other statements.

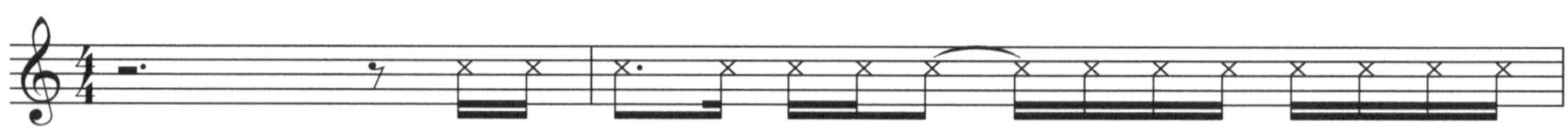

The rhythmic language presented in these lines is just as crucial as the pitch content. Internalizing rhythmic phrases that resonate with you and creating variations is a powerful way to build vocabulary and work on your feel.

Here are examples of how the phrase could be looped to create three, four, five, and seven-beat cycles.

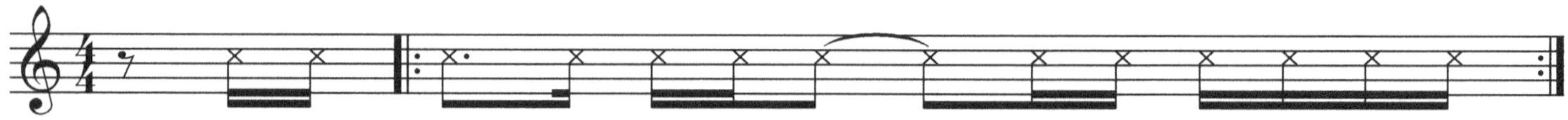

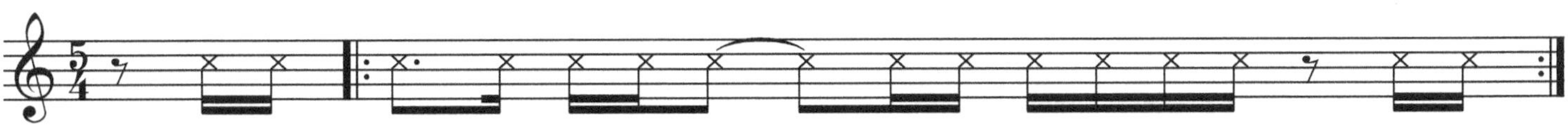

Line 21

♩ = 256 Source: Softly, as in a Morning Sunrise

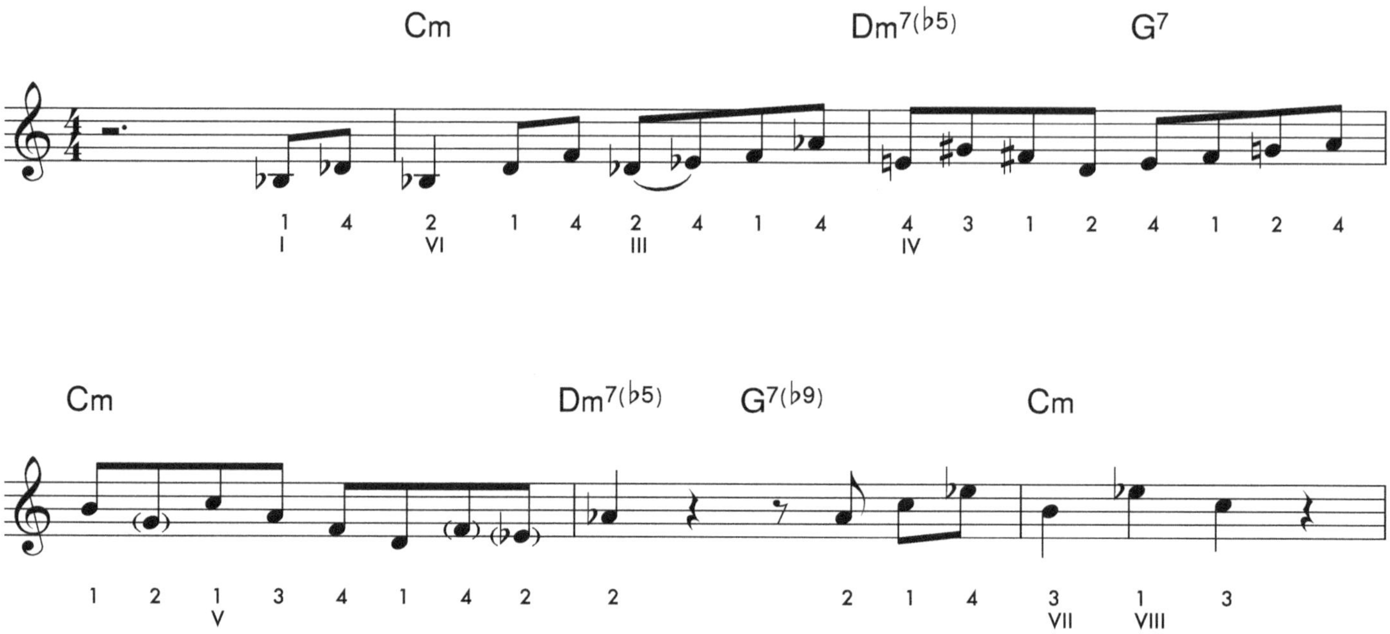

Line 21 Notes

A significant part of what drives the feeling of this line is the unique way that the fingerings shift from idea to idea. Sound and feel are the priority, rather than ease and efficiency. While these goals are not mutually exclusive, by directing the intention toward the sound and feel, you may discover ways of playing contrary to the approach found in more conventional guitar pedagogy.

Many fingerings are dictated by what precedes or follows a given phrase. So, changing even one note in a line can completely alter the direction of the selected fingerings.

To gain a greater appreciation for the unique fingerings used in this line (and other lines in this book), try taking a single idea and exploring various ways of playing that idea. Would you have made the same decisions? Why or why not? How does the feeling created by the original fingering compare to others? Is the "easiest" way the "best" way?

Here is the original fingering for the last phrase of this line.

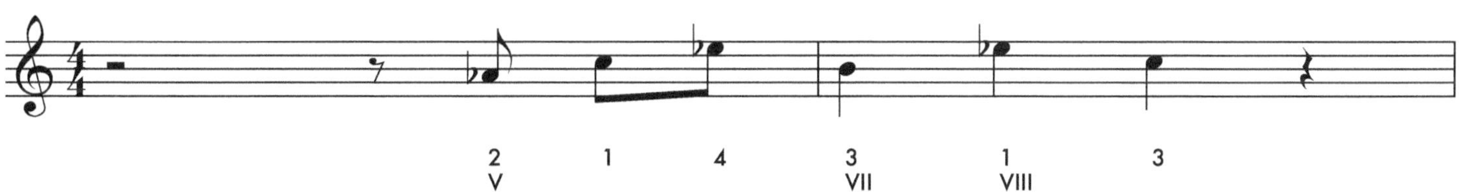

Here are some alternative fingerings for the phrase.

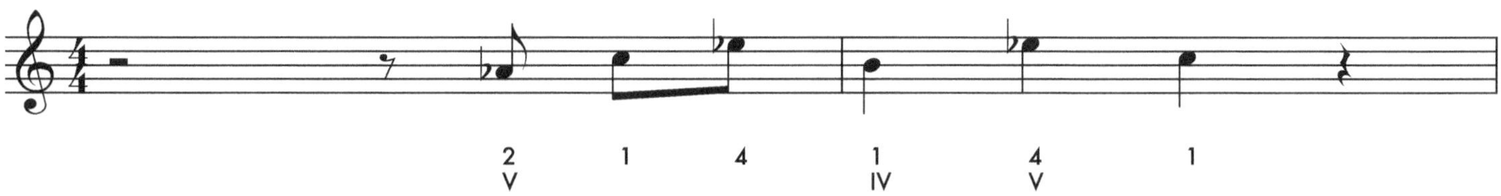

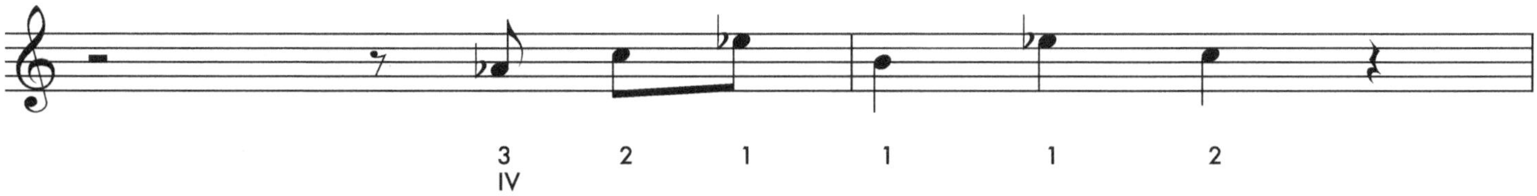

4 3 1 2 1 1
VIII V

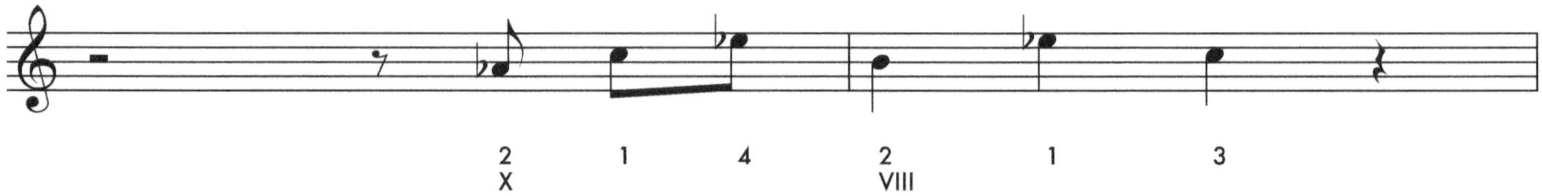
2 1 4 2 1 3
X VIII

2 1 1 2 1 2
X XIII VIX

Line 22

♩ = 114

Source: Blues in F

Line 22 Notes

The first half of this line is built off of minor triads played in ascending minor thirds.

This device is comprised of triads (three notes) played in a duple subdivision (sixteenth notes). So, each repetition of the minor triad starts one sixteenth note earlier than the previous, creating phrasing with a natural accent pattern and the feeling of falling back as you play forward in time.

Note that each transposition of the minor triad is played with the same fingering (1 4 3), necessitating shifts in position.

Here is an example that creates an exercise loop from this device.

Experiment with moving different types of triads (major, augmented, diminished, etc.) in minor thirds. Try moving any collection of pitches in minor thirds.

Line 23

♩ = 114 Source: Blues in F

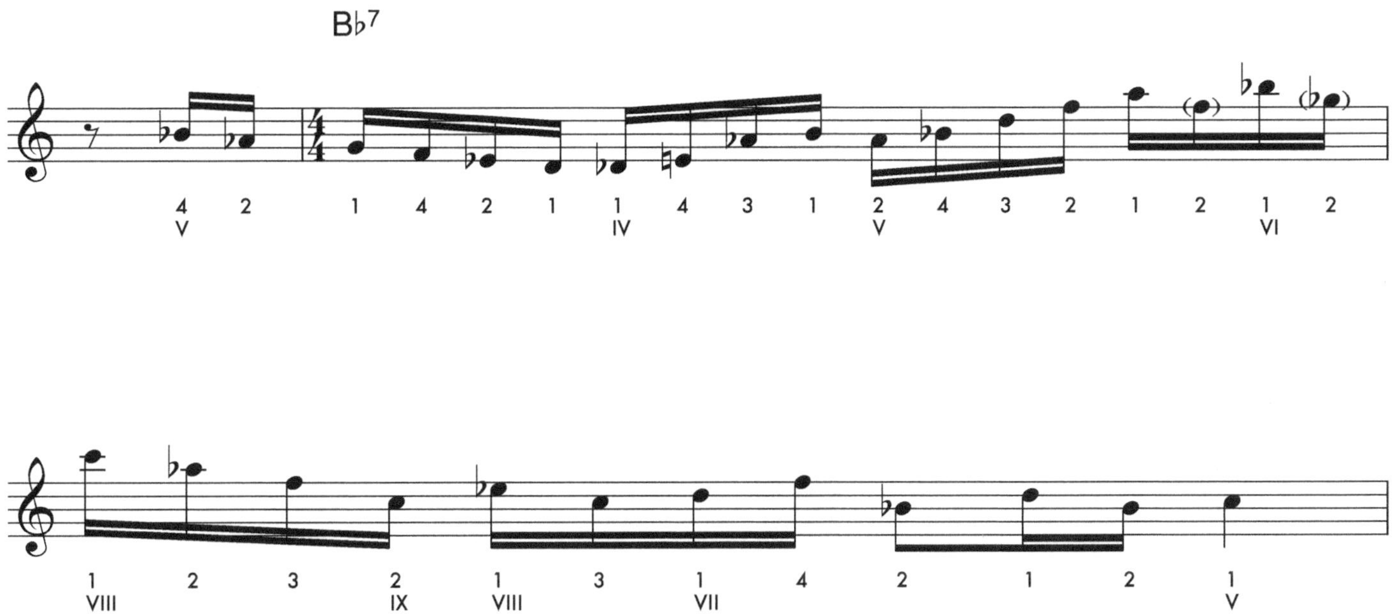

Line 23 Notes

This line contains subtle forms of sonic trickery that help to break away from predictability. By utilizing familiar phrases and shapes, but placing them in unexpected ways or altering them to break the typical pattern, it is possible to create a dual feeling of strength and assuredness, as well as exploration and mystery.

The first phrase of the line uses a familiar cadential idea. But instead of resolving into the target chord of B♭7 (the IV chord on an F blues), it appears to be resolving a fourth above into E♭7, only to change course again into an ascending D♭ minor seven arpeggio.

The next shape is a B♭ major arpeggio that begins on the ♭7th and ends on the natural 7th.

As an alternative approach to practicing arpeggios, try altering the arpeggio with each octave repetition or playing different variations ascending and descending.

Here are two example exercises incorporating this idea. The notation presents the basic material, which could be felt and played in many ways. The point of doing exercises like this is not to master and rehearse a new pattern to perform as written but to encourage exploration, introducing change into familiar patterns.

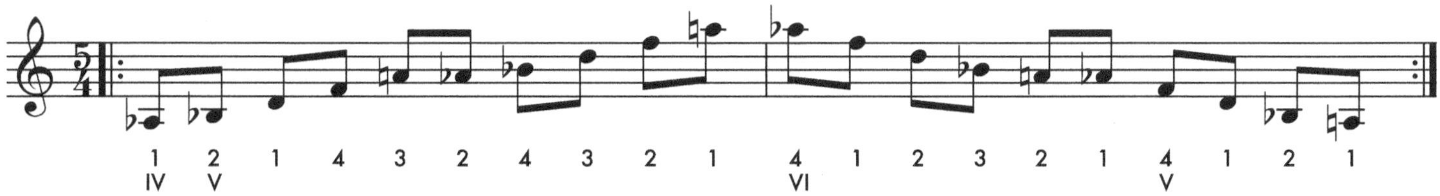

Line 24

♩ = 114

Source: Blues in F

Line 24 Notes

This line uses a tritone substitution (F♯-7/B7) to resolve from F7 to B♭.

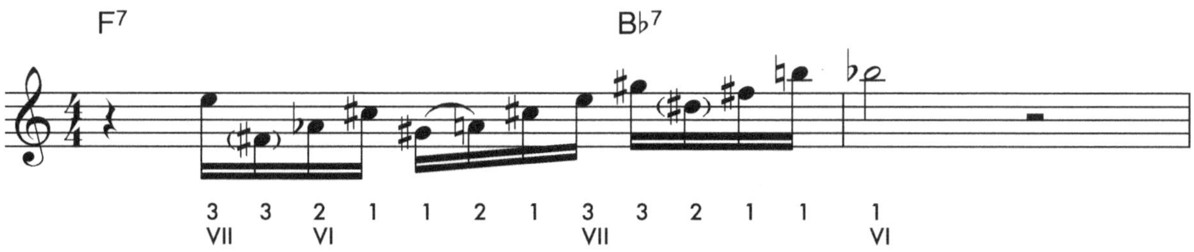

All of the notes in this device are diatonic to the key of E major. This is a reminder that the context in which you play something is crucial in determining how it will be perceived. If the underlying harmonic movement of the bass was B7 to E, then the feeling of dominant to tonic resolution would be completely unaltered. However, in the context in which it was played here (F7 to B♭7), it draws out altered colors on the F7 dominant chord (♭9, ♯9, ♯11, ♭13).

Notice how the first three notes of this line draw a melodic figure from a physical chord shape on the guitar, a standard fingering for an F-7 chord.

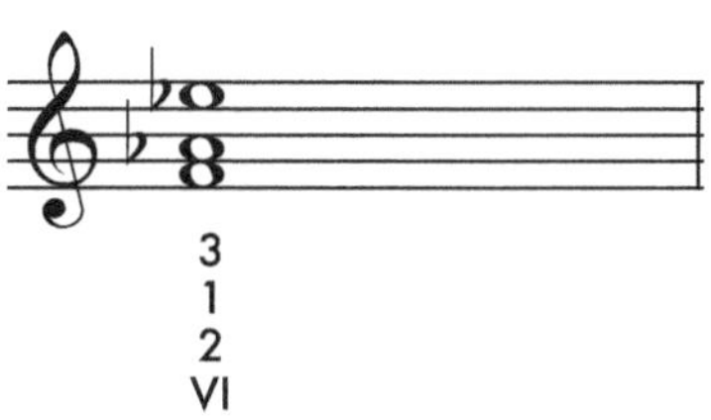

Taking chord shapes that you would typically use for comping and separating the notes to create melodies is a powerful device that utilizes the physicality of the instrument with forms that are already likely under your fingers.

Here is an example exercise using this physical chord shape to play through the form of Giant Steps. Try taking any familiar chord shape and playing it through a tune or harmonic structure. Be open to not fitting every note as "correct" within the changes. Use your ears and intuition. Sometimes it is the integrity of the shape itself and how it is being manipulated that creates the impact of the device, rather than every note being harmonically justified. Also, try using the same shape but changing the order of the pitches.

Line 25

♩ = 234

Source: D Minor Blues

Line 25 Notes

This line includes shifts guided by the strength of each individual melodic cell. Many exercises and improvisational challenges can be generated by looking closely at where and how these shifts occur and grappling with the mechanical consequences of these choices.

Here are some examples looking at phrases, drawing out principles that could be used as the seeds for further exploration, and creating exercises to get the device into your ears and hands. Remember, the example exercises below are only a sample of countless variations that could be generated using the examined principles. Use these examples as a guide for drawing your own conclusions and creating further exercises and variations.

Notice the two shifts in position in this phrase, first, a shift on the B♭ to play it with the third finger, and immediately following to play A natural with the first finger. Although playing a half step (B♭ to A) with two adjacent fingers may seem more obvious, notice how natural it feels to play with the fingering as written, especially when considering the overall motion of the line.

Here is an exercise that explores shifting this phrase one fret higher and lower than the original iteration of the idea. By practicing this eight-note phrase in triplets, you are also developing the ability to hear and feel this idea starting and ending on different parts of the beat, which is crucial to using the device spontaneously. Once you get the feel of moving this device around, try playing it on different string sets, altering the pattern, and deviating further from the original idea, using intuition as your primary guide.

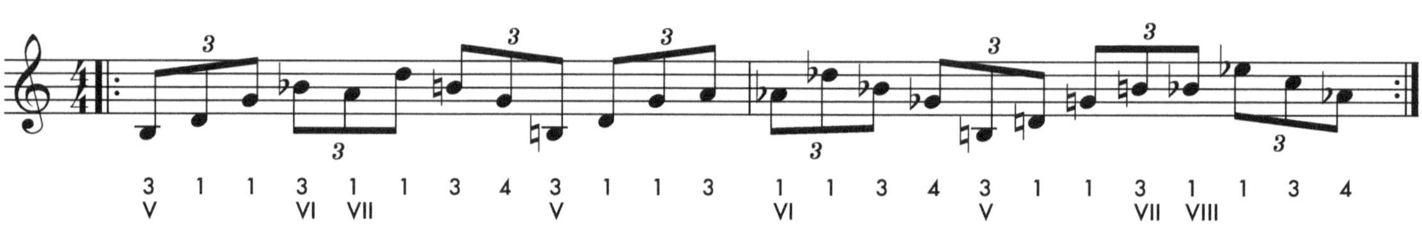

This phrase is built from two cells, each with four notes. Again, the way that these melodic shapes physically manifest contains clues worthy of contemplation.

Although the second A in the phrase could be played easily using the first finger, it is played with the fourth finger instead, requiring a shift in position. The choice is motivated by the physical integrity of the following four-note cell rather than the smoothness of the transition from note to note.

Here are three example exercises that explore some of the ways that these shapes could be moved around. Also, practice these exercises starting on the upbeat and in different subdivisions. These examples represent only a minimal view of the harmonic possibilities generated by moving and combing these two cells in various ways. Consider spending an entire day contemplating just these two shapes and applying them on harmonic structures and tunes you are practicing.

Line 26

♩ = 114

Source: Blues in F

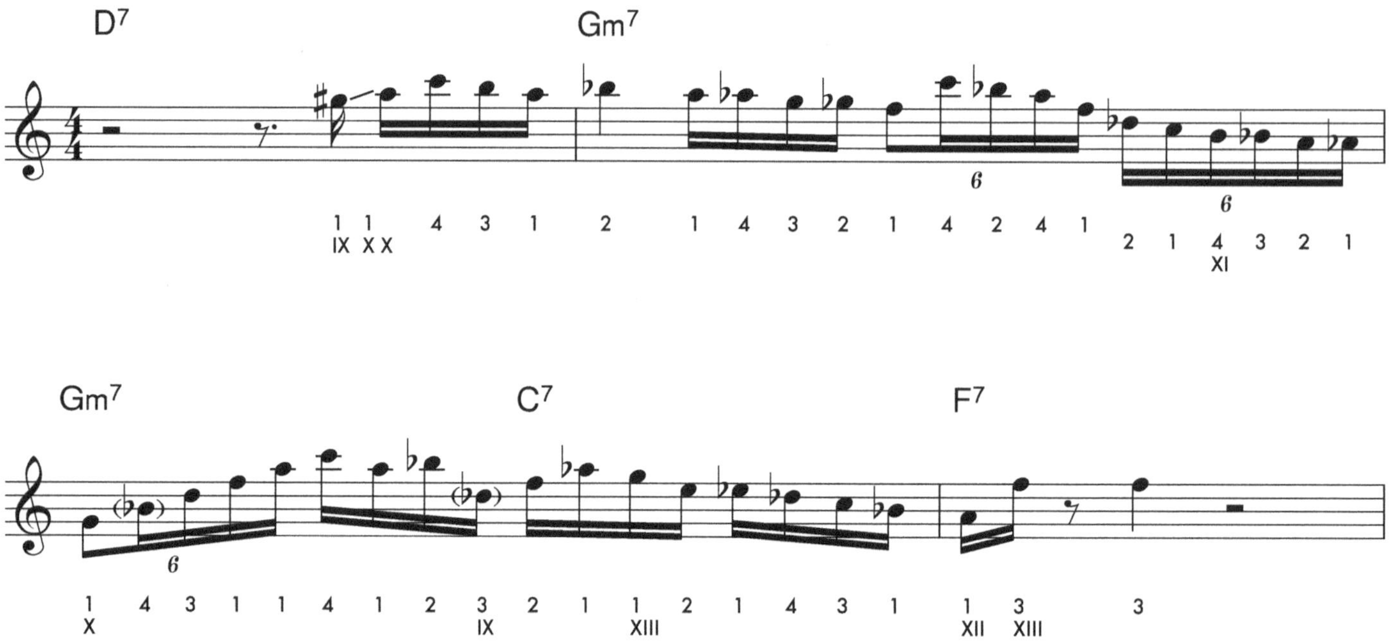

Line 26 Notes

The first phrase in this line is a chromatic enclosure targeting the minor third of the target chord, Gm7. Applying this device to target all of the chord tones in a given chord can help you see and hear the chromatic connective tissue between and around the notes in a chord.

Here is an example that uses the device to target all of the chord tones in Gm7. Once you get this under your fingers, use the same principle to apply the enclosures on various common chords (minor, major, augmented, diminished, seventh chords, etc.)

These examples represent the basic pitch material, notated with no slurs, slides, or ghost notes. Try using different approaches to picking, slurring, and sliding to get the vibe you are hearing. Although the example is notated in just one octave, practice these shapes throughout the instrument, experiment with different fingerings and connect the device to other musical material.

Another crucial aspect of this line is how it navigates between two rhythmic strata. Moving between sixteenth notes and double-time triplets (sextuplets) creates a feeling of accelerating and decelerating.

Here is an example exercise using only chromatics to practice switching between sixteenths and sextuplets. This is a starting point to get comfortable moving around the instrument, feeling the different subdivisions, and transitioning between them. Next, try applying the same concept in a less restricted improvisatory sense and with material and devices in your vocabulary.

The exercise is notated as a reference to get the idea. First, get a sense of the movement from the written material, then use it as a basis for further practice and exploration.

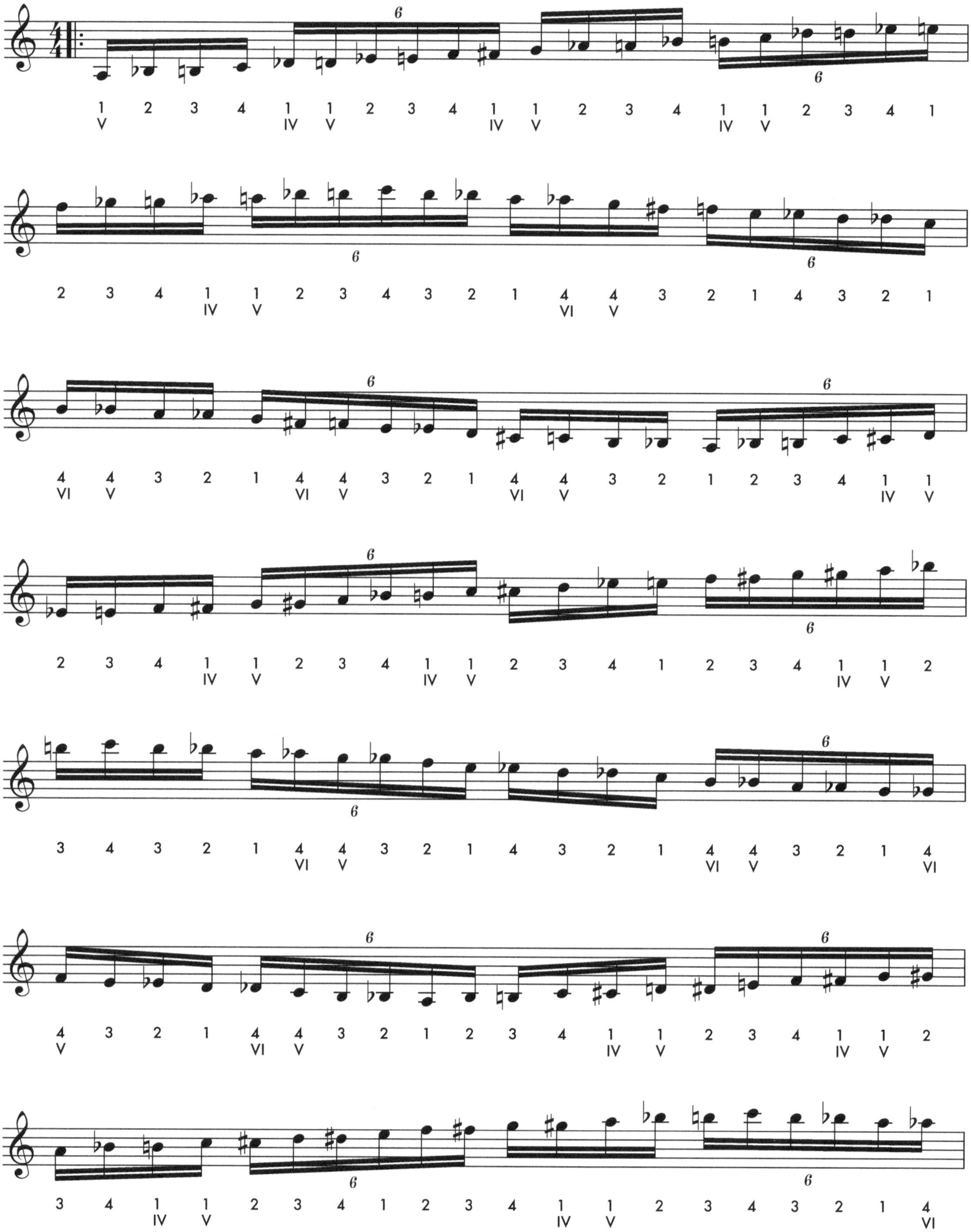

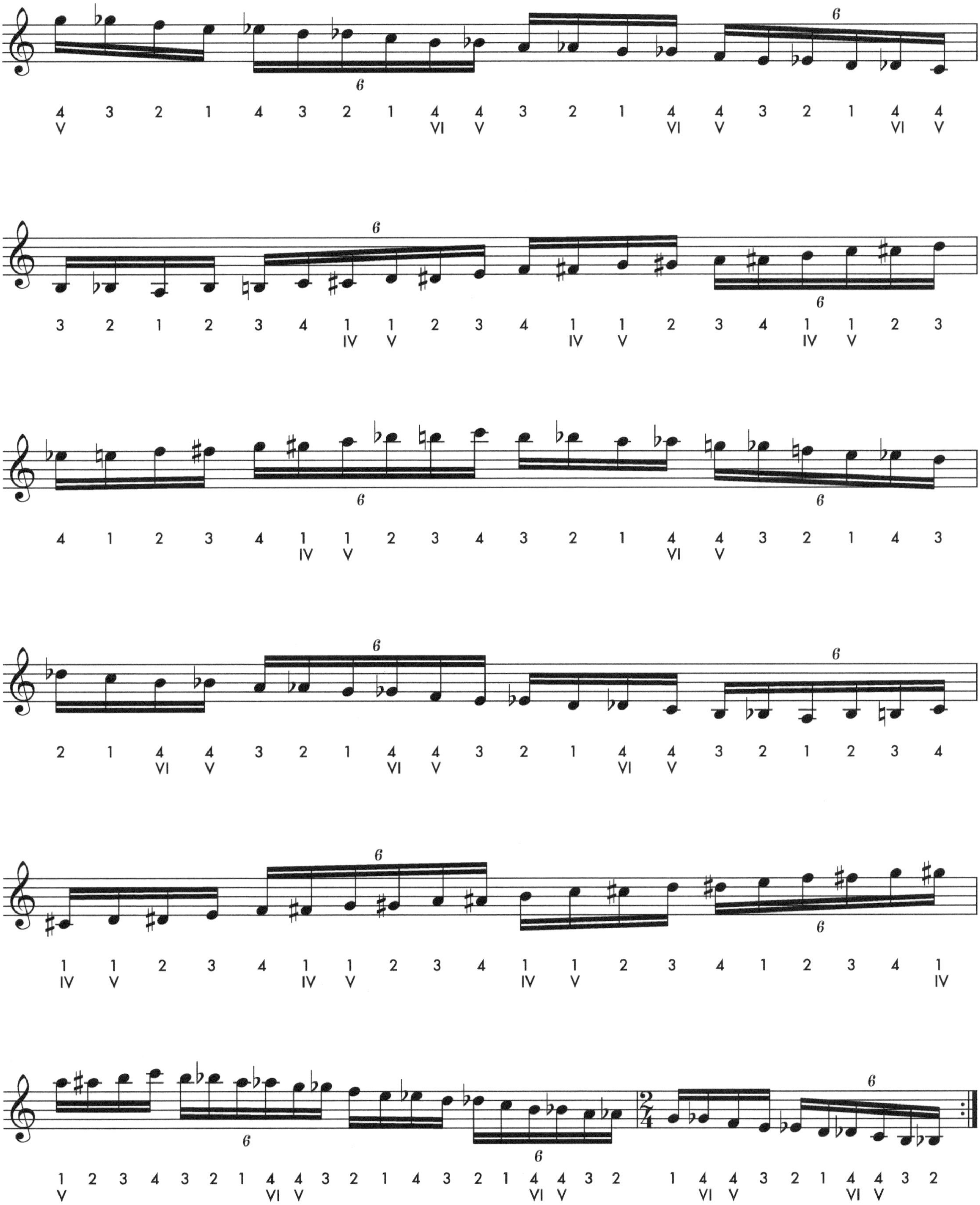
6 6
4 3 2 1 4 3 2 1 4 4 3 2 1 4 4 3 2 1 4 4
V VI V VI V VI V
6 6
3 2 1 2 3 4 1 1 2 3 4 1 1 2 3 4 1 1 2 3
IV V IV V IV V
6 6
4 1 2 3 4 1 1 2 3 4 3 2 1 4 4 3 2 1 4 3
IV V VI V
6 6
2 1 4 4 3 2 1 4 4 3 2 1 4 4 3 2 1 2 3 4
VI V VI V VI V
6 6
1 1 2 3 4 1 1 2 3 4 1 1 2 3 4 1 2 3 4 1
IV V IV V IV V IV
6 6 6
1 2 3 4 3 2 1 4 4 3 2 1 4 3 2 1 4 4 3 2 1 4 4 3 2 1 4 4 3 2
V VI V VI V VI V VI V

Line 27

♩ = 119

Source: Vamp in G minor and B♭ minor

Line 27 Notes

The basis for this line originates from the figure below, which condenses the cycle of fifths into a smaller range by changing direction, inverting some of the fifths to descending fourths. The figure includes all twelve chromatic pitches. Several musicians, including saxophonist Arthur Blythe and pianist Walter Bishop Jr., shared this concept and used it as a foundational element of their musical approach.

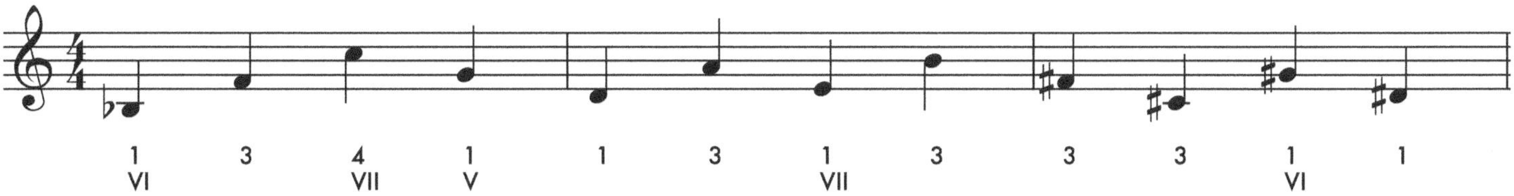

There are numerous ways to practice and apply this device, and many variations can be generated. Memorize the primary sequence and get it under your fingers. Then, experiment with creating rhythmic variations, applying the concept on tunes (consider starting with tunes that are more "modal" in nature), and melodic deviation from the pattern.

Here is the figure notated in a few different rhythmic subdivisions. In each subdivision, practice the figure starting on the different rhythmic partials.

Notice that because the figure has twelve pitches, the cycle repeats every three or six beats when played in a duple subdivision. In the context of a 4/4 meter, it is a helpful device for phrasing "over the barline."

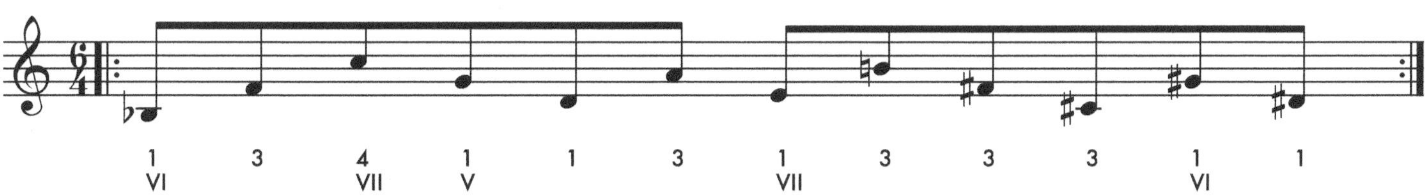

The way that this concept is realized in the context of this line is an expansion and variation of the original idea. Notice how the shapes in the line are derived from the fifths figure. Some of the directionality is altered, and the figure shifts while maintaining much of the physicality and melodic contour of the original shape.

Using your ear and intuition to guide you, use the physical and melodic principles that you absorb through practicing the basic figure along with the foundational rhythmic work of playing it in different rhythmic subdivisions and orientations as a point of focus in your improvisational practice.

To get a sense of some of the additional possibilities using this figure to derive new melodic shapes using similar physical forms, here are a few examples incorporating slight alterations to the direction and intervallic structure. The examples are notated in several rhythmic cycles to encourage you to develop variations using different feels and meters. The examples are notated in 4/4, 9/8, and 5/4 only for representational purposes. In a musical sense, applying ideas of varying lengths over a steady pulse or meter will help to create a stronger sense of phrasing.

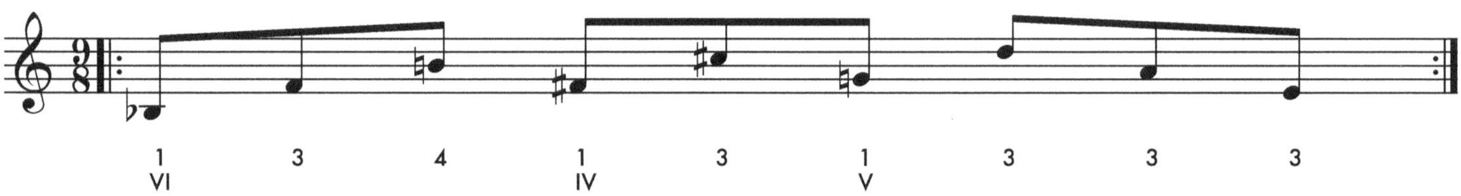

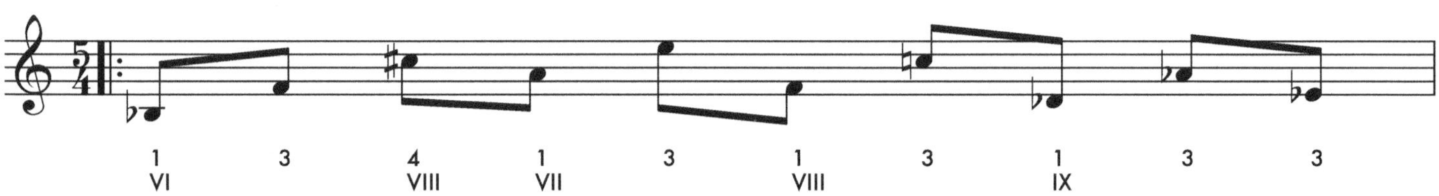

Line 28

♩ = 234

Source: D Minor Blues

Line 28 Notes

Using pitches only from the D minor pentatonic scale, this line creates movement and feeling through phrasing, combining melodic cells of differing lengths and directionality.

One way to contemplate the various phrases and how they combine is to break the line into shorter sections that can be repeated. Focus your attention on each phrase until you feel ready to add the following phrase in an additive process.

Here is one way to break down the phrases and play them additively. There are different ways of perceiving the phrases. You could also alter the subdivision or duration of any individual pitches or rests in each phrase. Experimentation is key. The exercise below is only a guide to breaking down and repeating phrases as a contemplative practice.

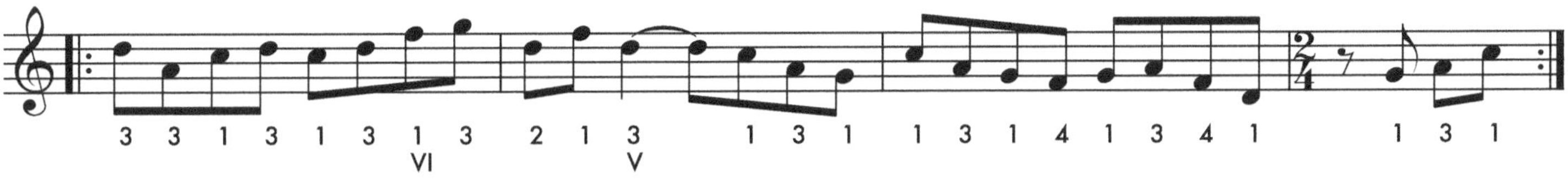

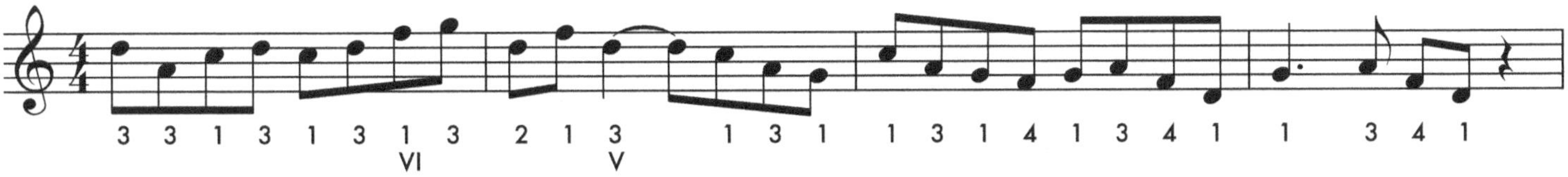

Notice how in bar three of the line, the D natural on beats one and two is played with a different finger each time. This is a subtle mechanical choice that impacts the way the next phrase sounds and feels.

Explore how changing fingers for a pitch played in a single location on the guitar can impact the sound and implicate alternative pathways.

Try using the example fingerings below as the starting point for launching various ideas, and consider the possibilities and directions that become available with each approach.

Line 29

♩ = 234

Source: D Minor Blues

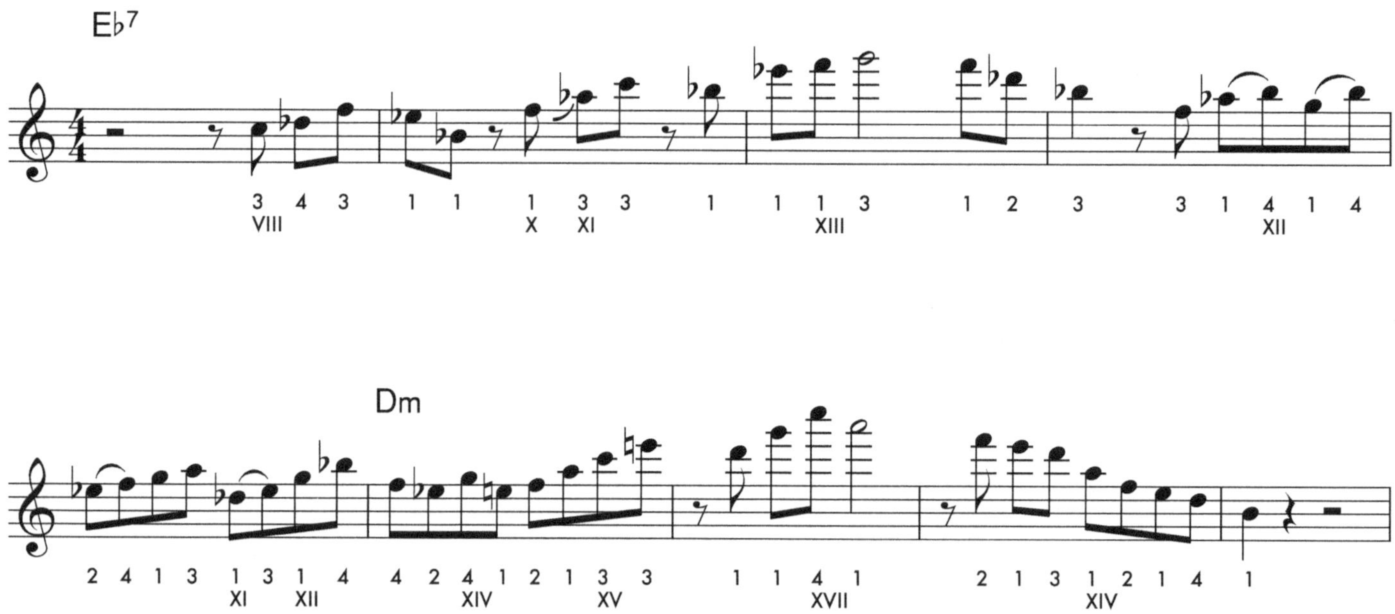

Line 29 Notes

Notice how the articulation of this line involves hammer-ons, notated as slurs. This approach contrasts with the sound of picking every note in a phrase and fosters natural dynamics.

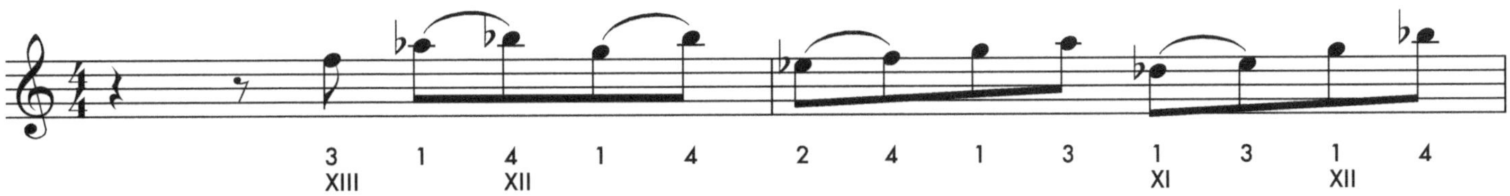

The first slur above is a hammer-on from the first to the fourth finger, but spanning only a whole step (A♭ to B♭) requires a position change. This shift is in preparation for the next pitch in the phrase, G, played with the first finger, and puts you in position for the subsequent sequence of pitches.

With this in mind, consider how this concept could be applied to shift in different ways. Here are some examples that hammer-on to the same note using different fingers. Each choice causes a chain reaction of possibilities. Try creating lines and variations launching from these examples. What are the results?

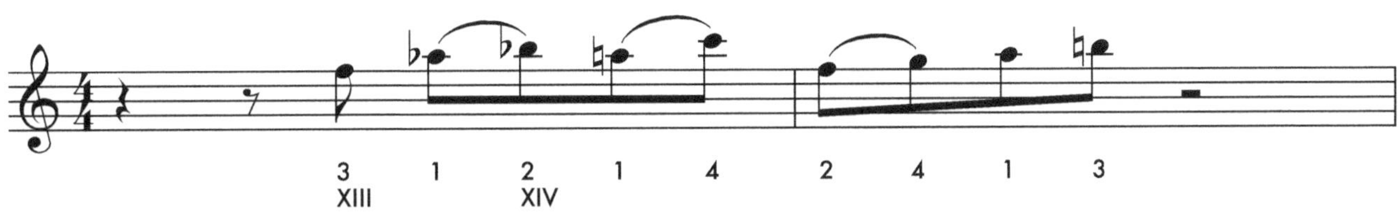

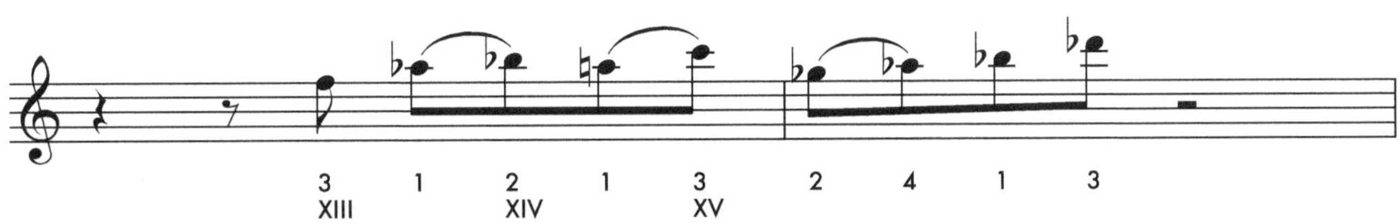

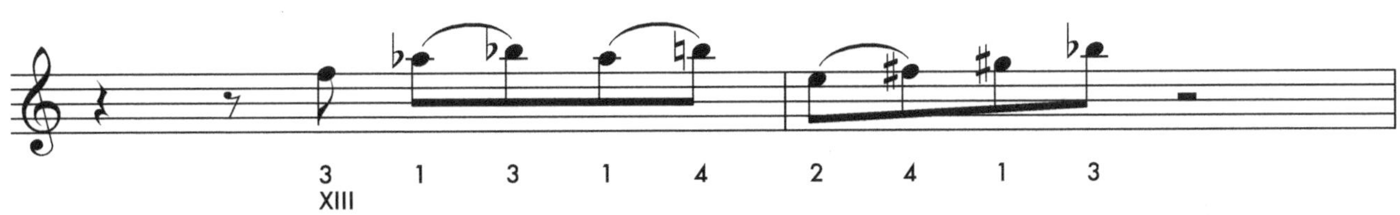

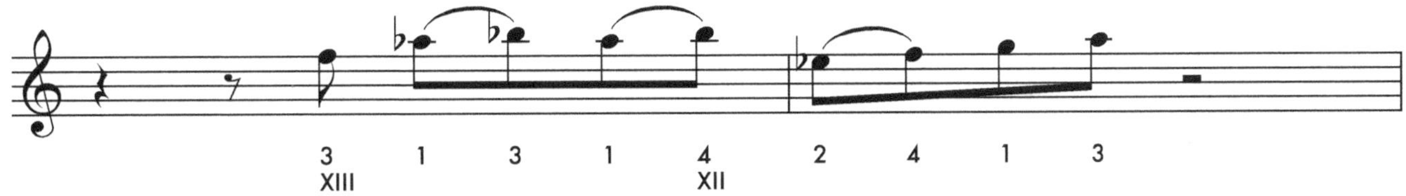

The first three bars of this line contain compact and conversational phrases. It is instructive to practice each of these phrases as loops, in their original form and shifted rhythmically, to gain greater control over the material and to explore how they feel on both sides of the beat.

The example exercise below creates loops out of the first four phrases in the line, suggesting one way of looping each phrase. Also, explore alternatives that modify the number of beats in each phrase, adding more or less space.

These ideas are consolidated into one bar cycles in different meters to represent them compactly in notation, not necessarily notated starting in the same part of the measure as originally played. Since this exercise is about getting a sense of alternating between starting phrases on downbeats and upbeats, concern yourself less with the resultant meter of the loop than the feeling created by shifting the idea rhythmically.

Line 30

♩ = 256

Source: Softly, as in a Morning Sunrise

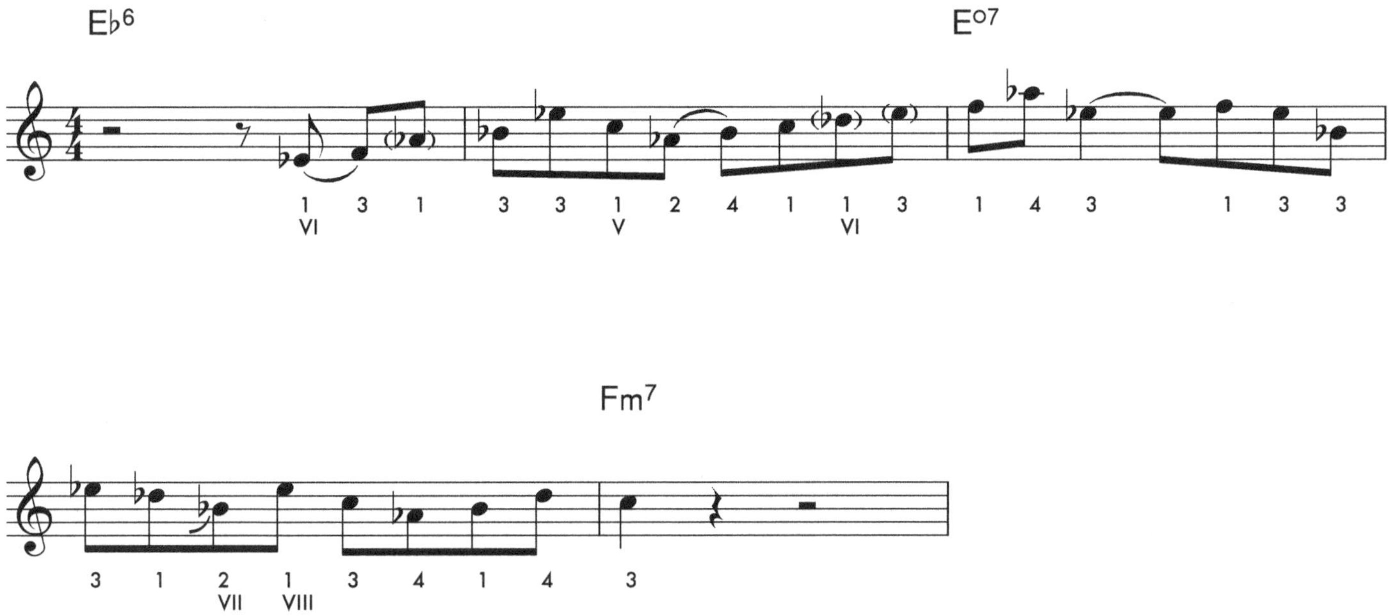

Line 30 Notes

The feeling of a phrase can be entirely altered by a subtle choice, like sliding into a note. The resulting impact on fingerings can change the directionality of an idea and the physical and melodic shapes that are most accessible. How you hear an idea and how it feels to play it on the guitar are interconnected in a constant feedback loop, each informing and supporting the other.

Here is a phrase from this line that illustrates this concept. Notice the shift in position on B♭ in the second bar of this example. Sliding into B♭ using the second finger causes a change in position and creates momentum for another quick positional change to play E♭ with the first finger.

To further explore the feeling created by this device, try building off of the momentum of a smaller section of the phrase to continue the idea through the range of the instrument. Here is an example exercise using the same fingering, starting on the high E string and repeating on each subsequent string set. Notice how as the phrase repeats, the pitch content trends lower while your position on the instrument trends higher. What is the feeling created by this cross current? Because of the nature of the guitar's tuning, the melodic shapes resulting from this physical movement's repetition differ depending on the string set. Rather than trying to "correct" for this phenomenon, try embracing it and learning to use the variety of melodic material potentially generated from a single type of movement.

This example is only one possible way of expanding upon this type of movement. Also, try using the device improvisationally on tunes and in different harmonic situations.

Line 31

♩ = 264

Source: Blues Minor

Line 31 Notes

Look closely at the rhythmic punctuation of this line. Focusing your attention on where phrases end and the rhythmic figures created by those landings can give you another way of understanding and using space, melodic and rhythmic grammar, and phrasing.

Here is one way of perceiving the points of rhythmic punctuation, shown by the arrows.

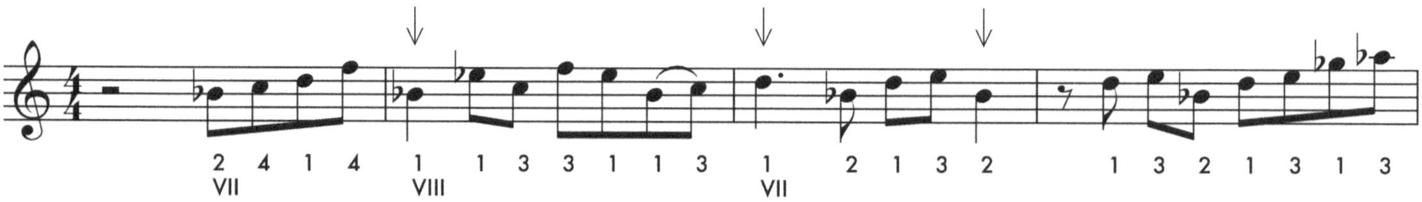

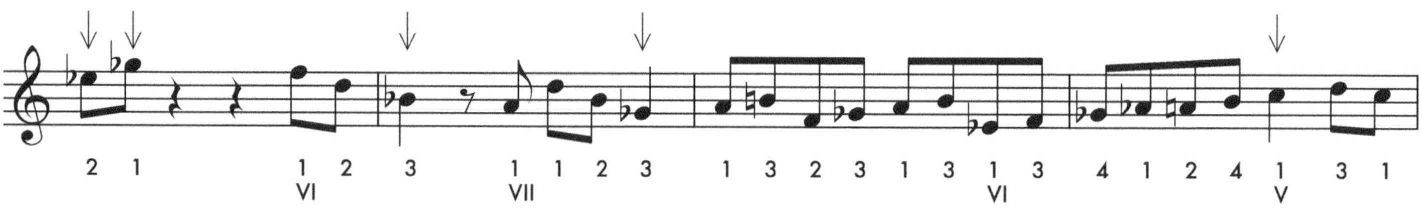

As an exercise, internalize the line above and practice hearing it against the rhythmic framework created by the phrases, playing the line and tapping the rhythm with your foot, or singing the line (with pitches or only rhythms) while clapping the rhythm. Also, repeat the melody in your mind while clapping the rhythmic figures.

Line 32

♩ = 264

Source: Blues Minor

Line 32 Notes

Notice how the phrases in this line are built on beat patterns of varying lengths, creating rhythmic structure and a sense of forward momentum that is not rigidly attached to the underlying 4/4 meter.

The first two phrases of the line are each six beats long, a total of twelve beats, or three bars in 4/4 time. Besides a pickup note on the first phrase, the two ideas are rhythmically identical. Consider how the phrasing of this line creates layers of rhythm and structure. What musical ideas can be generated by exploring the relationships between three, four, six, and twelve?

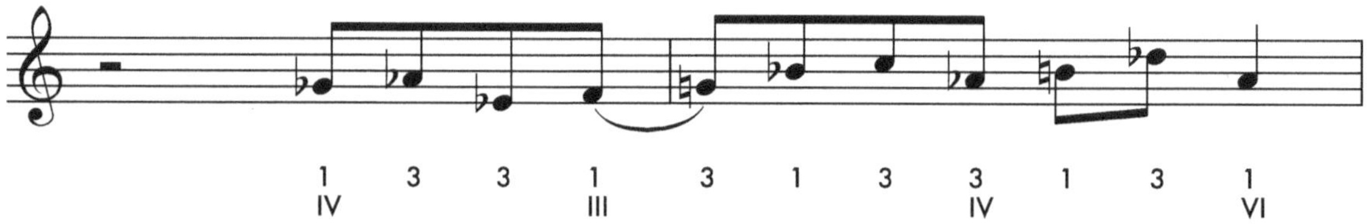

One way to work on hearing six-beat phrases against a 4/4 beat is to repeat a six-beat rhythm while counting in 4/4. Practice this using the melodic content of the phrases above and isolated as rhythms, playing on one note or improvising various melodic ideas using rhythmic ideas from the phrase.

Counting aloud is one mechanism for keeping yourself honest and learning to hear different rhythms over a repeating structure, but it is only one tool available to develop this skill. Here are some other ideas to practice developing this skill.

Practice the phrase over a drum track or backing track of a blues or any other tune, focusing on how the rhythmic orientation changes as it is repeated or transformed.

Practice repeating a phrase while singing or tapping another rhythm in a static beat cycle. Here are two examples of this idea below, using rhythms that fit in a four-beat cycle.

To further your rhythmic flexibility and ability to hear phrases in different ways, repeat all of the example exercises above, shifting the phrase by an eighth note to start on the upbeat.

Start by counting in 4/4 while playing the shifted phrase, then sing various rhythmic figures four beats in length while playing the shifted phrase. All of this work will contribute to developing a sense of rhythmic stability.

Here is an example of the shifted phrase played against the same underlying rhythmic figure as above. The notation is a guide for understanding the premise of the exercise, but you will get the most benefit when you internalize the figures and practice without reading. Once you can play the phrase with these example rhythms, develop variations to advance your ability to hear it against various rhythms.

Line 33

♩ = 264

Source: Blues Minor

Line 33 Notes

The first phrase of this line is a fundamental dominant to tonic resolution. While it is played here on a B♭ minor chord, it is anticipating the resolution to the tonic key of the tune (Blues Minor), which is in the key of F minor. Memorize this phrase and practice it in all keys, in various locations, and string sets on the guitar. Then, as this line demonstrates, consider how this idea can be placed in different ways, both rhythmically and harmonically, to create different types of tension and melodic and tonal relationships.

Here is the simplified, basic version of the idea. Explore alternate fingerings and practice creating variations.

This line uses figures based on minor tonalities played in various relationships (major thirds, minor thirds, and whole tone). In the line itself, the phrases include chromatic and scalar connective tissue. The example below is simplified, notating all the shapes as minor seventh arpeggios. Also, explore these relationships using other formations. Start with various types of minor arpeggios (minor triads, minor sixth, minor major seventh, etc.) Try various fingerings.

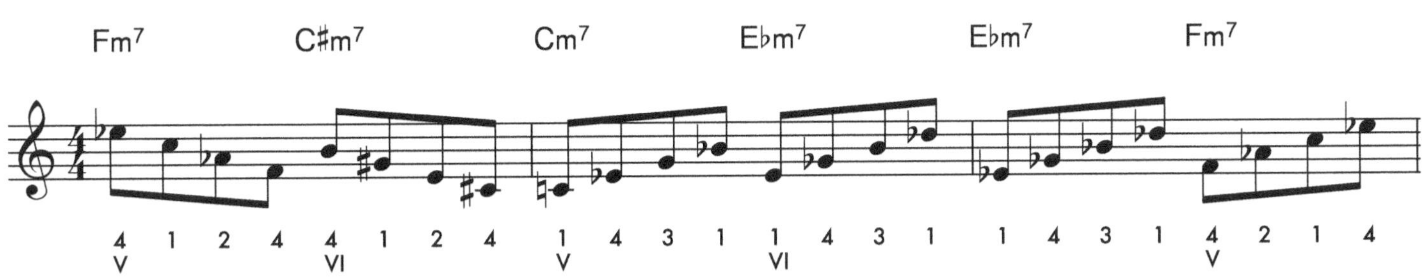

Here is an example exercise drawing upon these three relationships (major thirds, minor thirds, and whole tone), extending the pattern to cover a fuller range of the instrument. The same principles explored in this exercise can be applied to any arpeggio or pitch formation (cells, scales, melodic phrases from various sources).

As a way of further exploring these relationships, try extending lines that you already know. Here is an example using this line, expanding it by continuing the minor seventh arpeggios moving in minor thirds up the octave, leading to the closing phrase of the original line played up an octave.

Line 34

♩ = 234

Source: Blues in F

Line 34 Notes

This line includes fundamental blues language, using a particular way of articulating and sliding into notes to bring a singing quality to melodic ideas. There are various ways of achieving this sound and feeling on the guitar, requiring experimentation and attention to detail to develop a personal approach.

The first two phrases of this line both slide into the downbeat. The first phrase slides from E♭ to F using the fourth finger, and the second slides from B♭ to C using the third finger.

Here is an example exercise that draws upon the approach of these two phrases, using the same devices, extending through the range of the instrument and F minor pentatonic tonality. There are many ways of applying these principles. Once you are familiar with the phrases and movements offered in this exercise, devise additional exercises and improvise using the devices to explore the possibilities.

Another subtle device that can impact the feeling of a line is ghost notes. In this phrase, there is a ghost note that is barely perceptible but has a tangible effect on how the idea sounds and feels.

Try removing the note to observe how the ghost note changes the phrase.

Try playing the phrase without ghosting the note, and observe the difference.

Here is an exercise that could be used as a warm-up for getting the feeling of this phrase under your fingers. Moving a figure around can help internalize an idea's physical lessons without mentally reinforcing that it "belongs" in a particular place on the instrument. This example moves in descending minor thirds but could be played in any interval or through chord changes. Apply the same principle on different string sets, exploring how you might have to alter the fingering to get a similar feeling.

Line 35

♩ = 234

Source: Blues in F

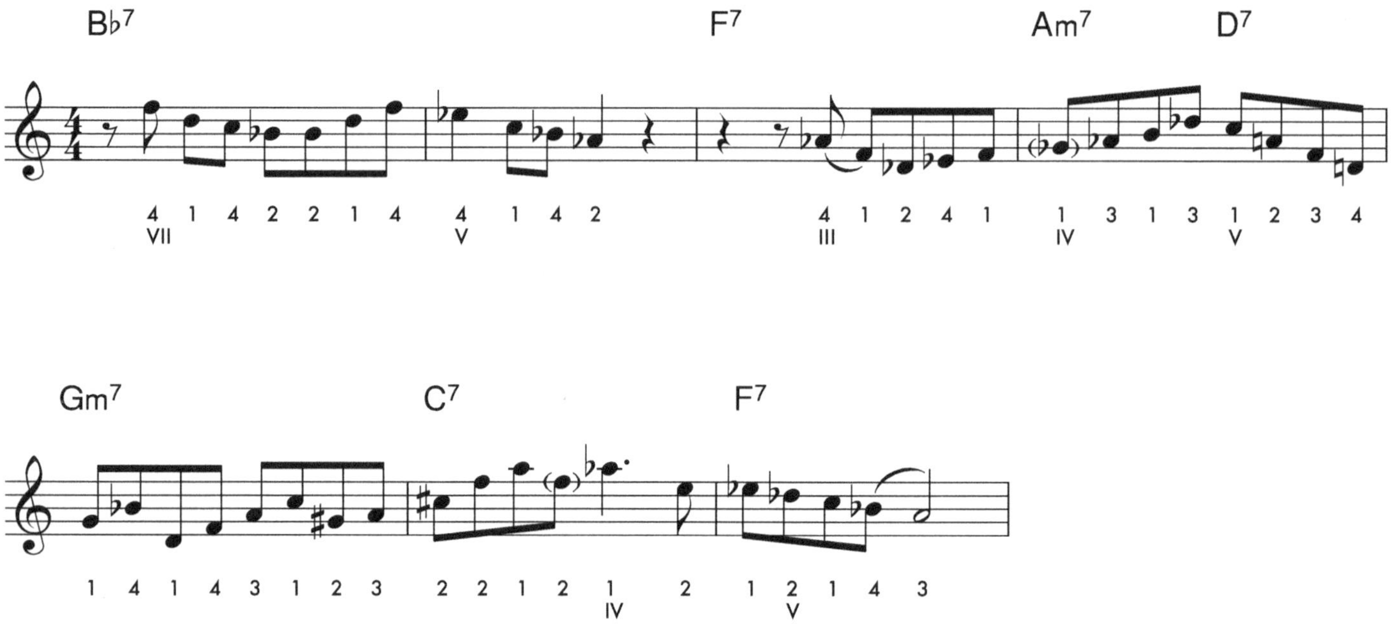

Line 35 Notes

The first three bars of this line are phrases based on this basic diatonic shape (1235) transposed into three tonalities (B♭, A♭, D♭).

The phrases draw on the same four-note pitch formation, each presented with distinct melodic and rhythmic information that can be studied.

Here are some example exercises to further explore the melodic and rhythmic ideas from the three figures above. Working on each idea through different transpositions and then recombining them in various ways is one approach that can be used to internalize the rhythmic and melodic language and learn to use it with greater flexibility.

These examples are only a guide. The notation represents some possibilities, but once you get the concept behind the exercise, it will be most effective to do this work without relying on the notation. Practice holding the three figures in your mind and playing them in different orders and transpositions. Work with the material in various ways and constantly push yourself to recontextualize and reexamine the ideas.

Line 36

♩ = 252

Source: Impressions

Line 36 Notes

All the phrases in this line are diatonic to the D minor tonality (Dorian mode) except the second phrase, a four-note whole-tone figure played descending, then ascending from a half step down.

Many devices and exercises can be generated by looking closely at this phrase. Its compact shape and the physical simplicity of the fingering create a solid framework for creating melodic and rhythmic variations.

Here are some suggested exercises. These variations are only a partial list of all possible permutations. Use this resource as a starting point for further exploration.

While these examples are notated as repeating four, five, and six-beat cycles, practice combining the figures in various ways to create additional rhythmic possibilities. Practice moving the shapes around in different intervals to explore harmonic and melodic possibilities. Consider and experiment with multiple approaches to articulating these devices (picking, slurring, ghosting, etc.). To discover further rhythmic options, play the phrases in different subdivisions, leave more or less space, and add or remove notes. Use your ear as your guide.

Line 37

♩ = 158 Source: Rhythm Changes

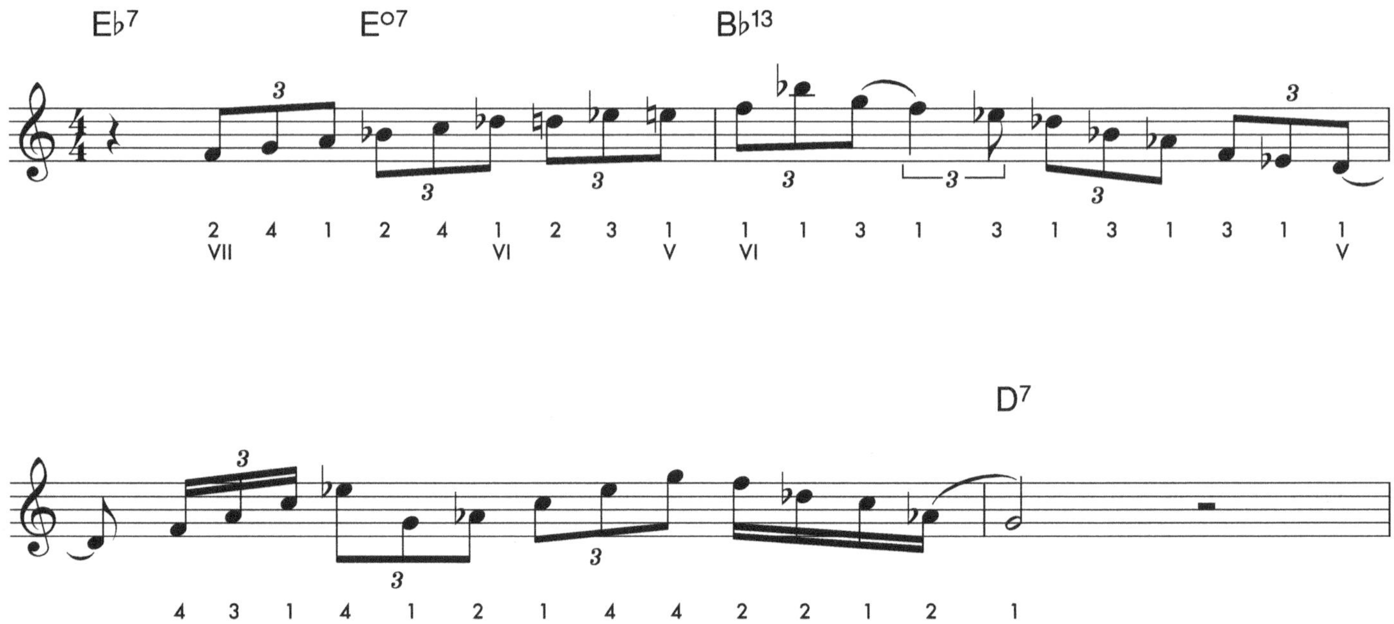

Line 37 Notes

This line is played in a triple feel, with a combination of eighth note and sixteenth note triplets. The first phrase of the line begins with a scalar passage, partially filled in with chromatics.

To develop control of how phrases can situate in different ways in a triple feel, try taking a single phrase and looping it. Here is an exercise based on the phrase above. Because the total length of the phrase is not divisible by three, the orientation to the beat will change with each repetition, cycling backward through the partials of the beat (first, third, second triplet).

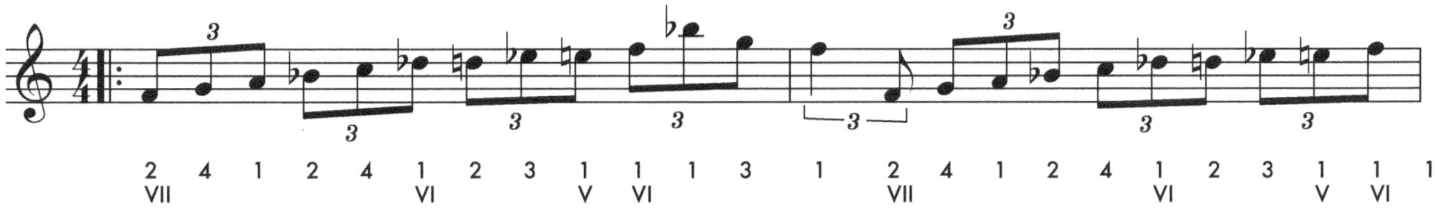

The last phrase of this line is a series of descending fourths, with approach notes from above leading into each note in the series, first a whole-step approach, then two chromatic approaches, leading into the downbeat of the bridge of rhythm changes.

Here is the underlying descending fourths structure.

Using the structure of fourths as a framework for expanding melodic ideas, here is an exercise approaching each note from above and below in various ways. This thought process could be applied to any structure. Because of the instrument's tuning, fourths are physically natural to the guitar and a compelling foundation to build upon for melodic exploration.

Building off the application of the concept demonstrated in Line 37, try combining different approaches (chromatic, whole step, minor third, etc.) The example exercise below combines various approaches in each series of fourths. Use the principles shown in these two examples to find other variations not notated here.

Line 38

♩ = 252

Source: Impressions

Line 38 Notes

This line is an example of directionalism, a technique where the pitch trends in one direction while your physical placement on the guitar moves in another. In this case, the phrases are trending downward in pitch while physically moving upward horizontally on the guitar.

In the context of this line, the dual movement occurs on a phrase-by-phrase basis. Notice how the positional shifts in this line also correspond to changes in tonality from phrase to phrase. Here is one way of perceiving the tonal movements of each phrase.

One way to practice this concept is to work on playing through a series of chords, navigating the changes while moving up or down the guitar neck following a physical shape. Here is an example exercise that moves through a chain of dominant chords through the cycle of fourths. The phrases trend downward in pitch while moving up on the guitar neck until reversing course and trending up in pitch and down on the guitar neck, repeating as many times as necessary to go through the entire cycle. As a demonstration, this example follows each chord change in a grid-like way, following each chord exactly as it changes on the beat. Once you get a sense of some of the possibilities using this type of movement, try applying the principle less rigidly, delaying or anticipating resolutions and varying the rhythmic vocabulary.

Another approach to practicing this way of moving on the instrument is to play a specific scale while limiting yourself to a certain number of notes per string. Here are a few examples of this approach using the chromatic scale. The same concept could be applied to any scale or melodic figure. Once you absorb some of the possibilities in the exercises, try combining scale fragments utilizing fingerings with a variety of notes per string. While practicing specific scales offers a map to begin exploring this device, try applying the general principles of movement that you discover from these exercises in a broader, improvisatory sense.

Chromatic scale, two notes per string

Chromatic scale, three notes per string

Chromatic scale, four notes per string

Line 39

♩ = 132

Source: F Minor Blues

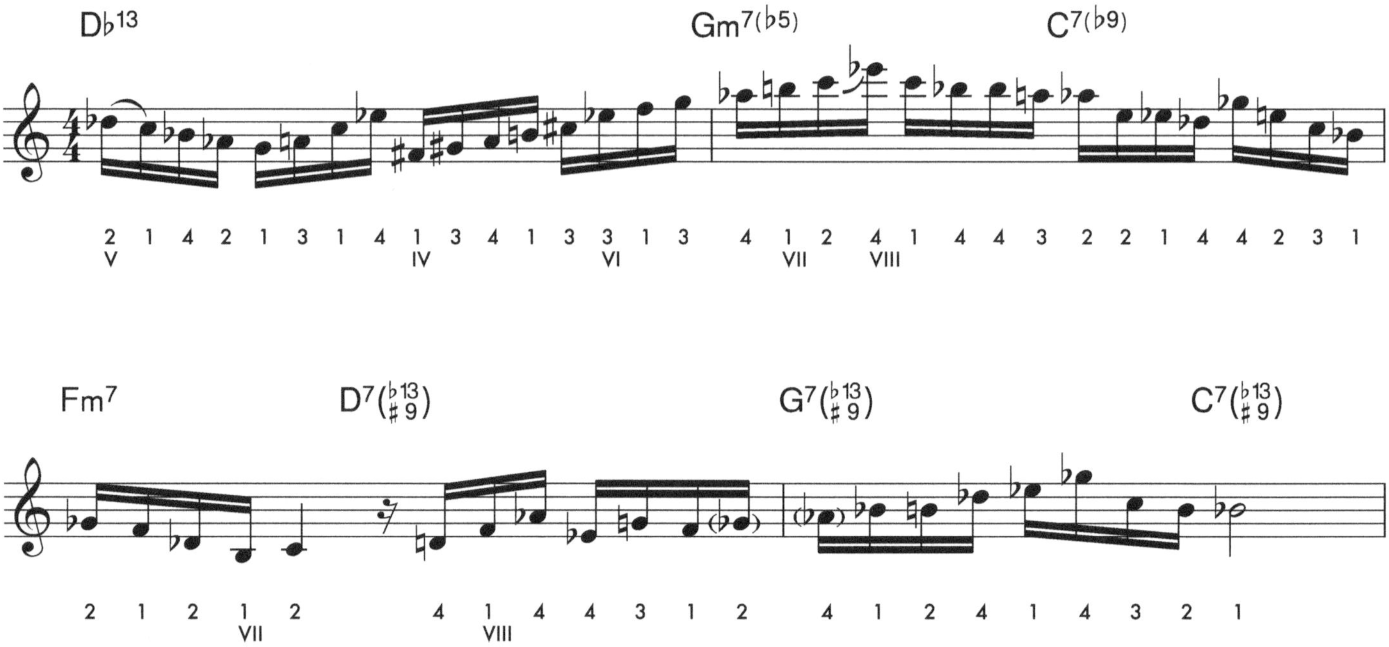

Line 39 Notes

This line begins with phrases that shift tonalities on almost every beat. Here is one way of perceiving the tonalities of the pitch collections.

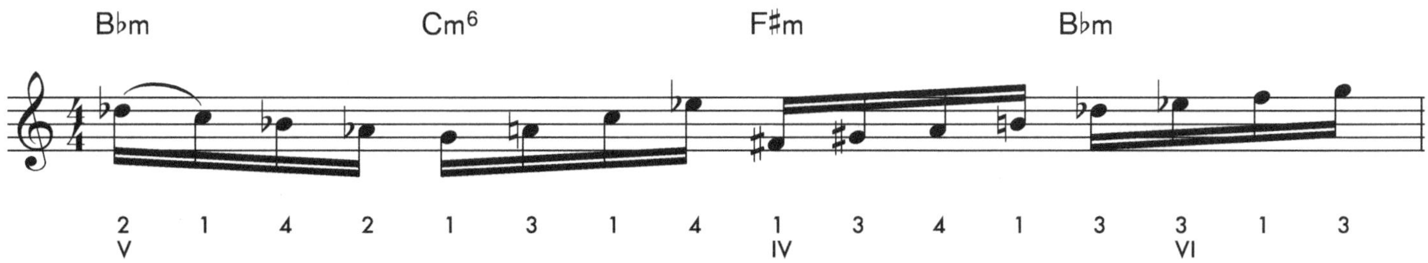

Often we study devices that correspond neatly to harmonic rhythms organized into two, four, three, or six-beat sections depending on a tune's underlying meter and structure. Introducing changes in tonality that occur at a faster rate can create a feeling of push and pull, generating a sense of excitement that is less common.

With this in mind, how could you devise musical exercises to develop this skill?

Here is an example exercise using shapes derived from minor tonalities, randomly changing tonalities on every beat, illustrating some possibilities you could generate using this approach. Also, try using harmonic structures and changes you already know, accelerating and recontextualizing them. Using randomness can be an effective way of pushing your mind beyond recycling old patterns. Let your ear guide your choices when applying these concepts to your improvisations.

To further develop your ability to hear and physically execute changes that expand upon or depart from the underlying harmonic rhythm, practice navigating through a tune using the technique demonstrated in the previous exercise. Try implying different harmonies on every beat, with awareness of the target chord changes that mark the form. There is no "wrong" way to do this if your intention is clear and you keep track of the underlying form. Here is an exercise that fills in a blues form with changes that depart from the core harmonic structure of the tune. This approach is related to the innovative way that Charlie Parker and Dizzy Gillespie improvised spontaneous harmonic pathways. Studying the movements they and others defined for us in their improvisations is essential to learning the nuances of the language. It is equally important to allow yourself to explore, aware of but untethered to any previous maps that influential musicians have left. This exercise is an example, not something to be memorized and rehearsed. Use the same process to select other pathways and improvise through them.

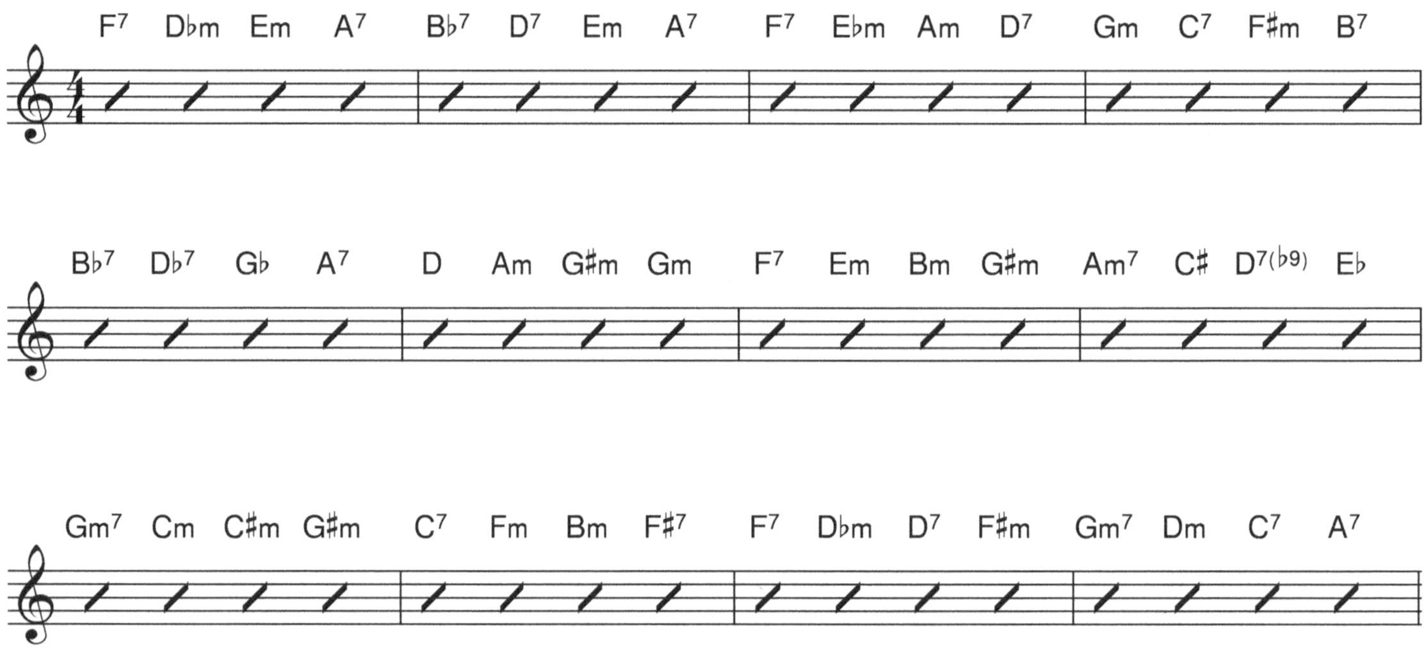

To be clear, the ultimate goal of this concept is not to play "random" chords through tunes but to free yourself to explore sounds you would not have found by using a purely "logical" process. Many choices may not sound good to you, but some will. Keep note of the movements that resonate with you and incorporate those into your vocabulary.

Line 40

♩ = 264

Source: Blues Minor

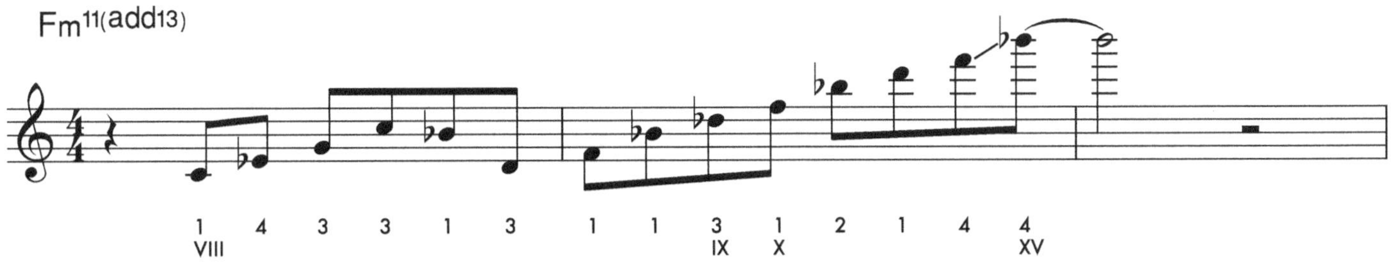

Line 40 Notes

This line is built from two triads, C minor and B♭ major, the v minor and IV major in the key of F minor. There is one exception, the D♭ on the second beat of bar two. Triad pairs draw out specific colors in a tonality and organize and structure these colors. While each note in the triads has a particular harmonic relationship to the tonality, we can build structures that can be expanded and moved in many different ways by organizing them into these familiar shapes. It is necessary to have a solid working knowledge of triads and inversions in all keys through the range of the instrument to apply this device.

Here are a few exercises using C minor and B♭ major, based on their application in Line 40. These exercises suggest ways to work with triads, moving the shapes through inversions, expanding one or the other of the triads, or changing direction in various ways. Once you try these, create additional variations and explore other triad pairs. Many different fingerings could work for these, and your choice of how to play them will be informed by the context and how the triads connect to other material in your improvisations.

Line 41

♩ = 133 Source: D Minor Vamp

Line 41 Notes

This line includes a device directly influenced by George Benson. There are many variations to this device. The basic gesture begins with a slide using the first finger and then an interval leap to an adjacent string. In this case, the interval leap is a sixth.

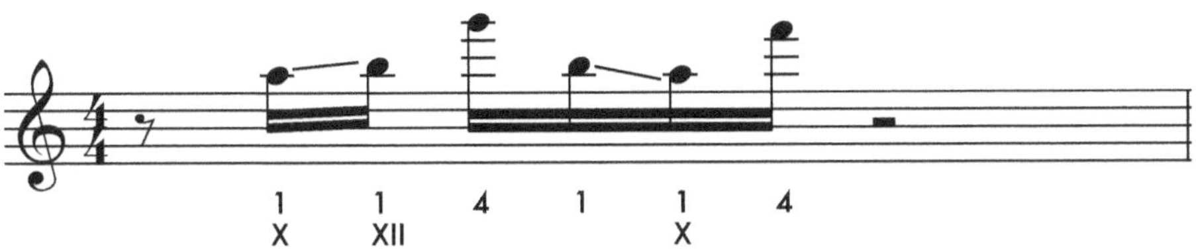

Because there are three notes in the figure, notice how it rhythmically shifts when repeated in a sixteenth or eighth note subdivision. Notice that in a sixteenth note subdivision, the phrasing implies a polyrhythm of four over three, and in an eighth note subdivision, two over three.

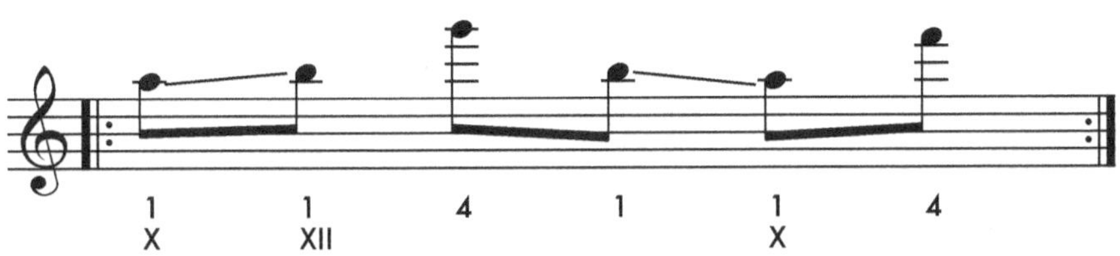

In Line 41, this device is moved around in whole steps, half steps, and minor thirds.

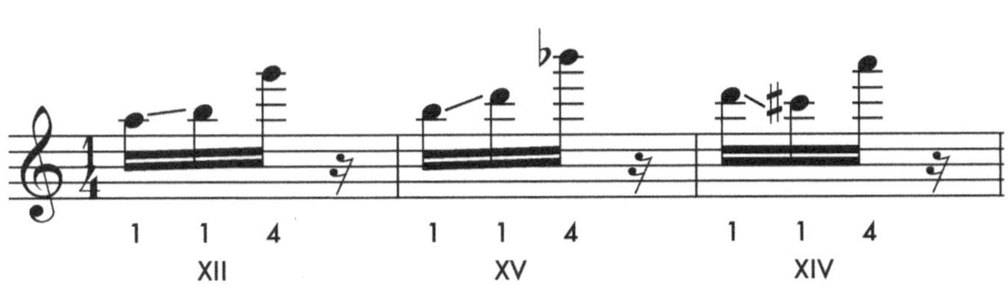

To explore some possible applications of the device, practice moving around in these three intervallic relationships (whole steps, half steps, and minor thirds), both ascending and descending. The examples notated here represent some possibilities using a limited range of a minor third for the distance between the first two notes in the phrase. Experiment with wider intervals and more extreme variations of the gesture as well.

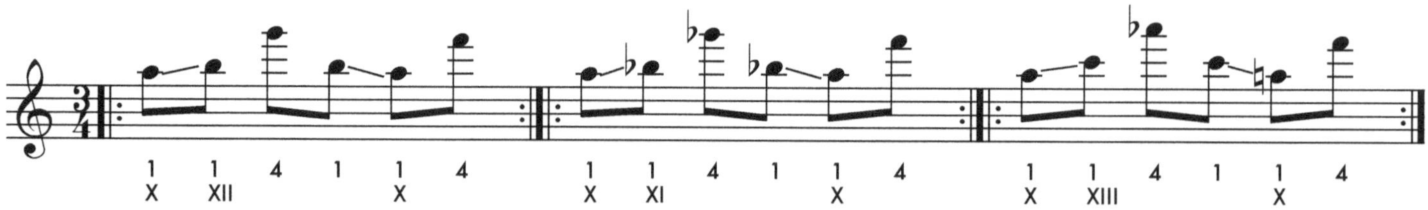

As demonstrated in Line 41, the application of this device calls for combining these variations to generate many types of movement. Here are some example exercises that combine two or more of the variations above, alternate ascending or descending patterns, or repeat a gesture.

To generate even more possible variations using this gesture, use the same principles of movement shown in the previous examples but alter the interval leap of the third note in the figure to make a fifth, tritone, or fourth. More variations can be created by skipping strings, changing the direction of the gesture to slide on the higher string, adding notes, leaving more space, etc.

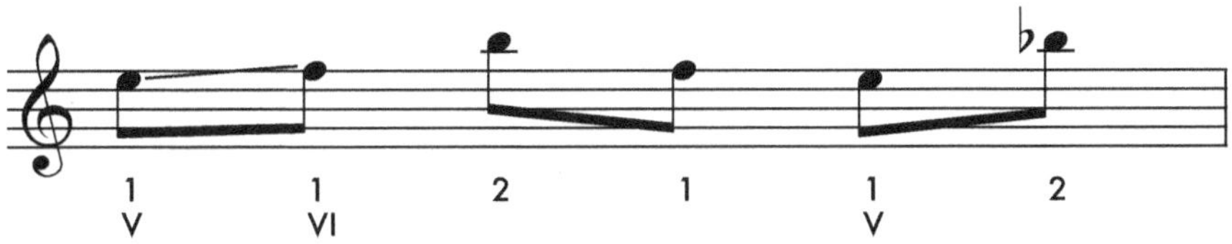

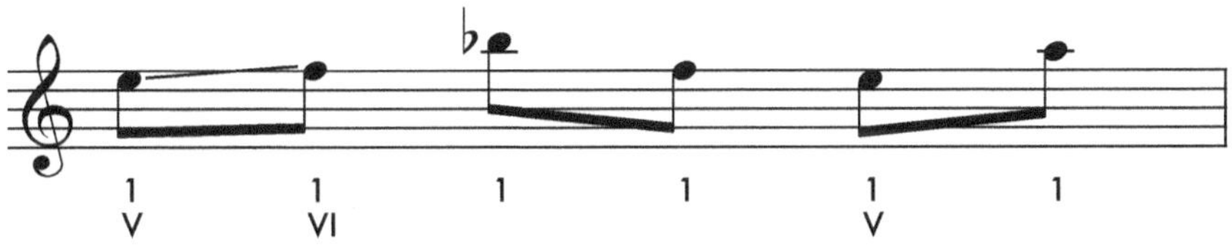

Line 42

♩ = 122 Source: Blues in G

Line 42 Notes

This line demonstrates the importance of understanding fundamental diatonic melodic sequences and arpeggios and the variety of ways they can be applied.

This line can be perceived as being built on diatonic shapes in the keys of E♭ major and G major. The shapes generated from E♭ major are applied over an E7 chord, functioning as a tritone substitution (F-7/B♭7 over E7). The last phrase is generated from G major, anticipating and targeting the II chord of a blues in the key of G.

The first phrase includes a diatonic sequence often used as a form of punctuation, a clear way of introducing, breaking up, or closing a statement. This phrase also leaves room for a response from the rhythm section and chordal comping on the guitar.

Here is the same phrase notated in an eighth note subdivision.

Practice this phrase in all keys throughout the range of the guitar, and explore alternative fingerings. It is a foundational idea that can be applied and varied in many ways.

Practice the phrase through tunes. First, apply it sequentially through chord changes, then work on varying the rhythm, playing it in different harmonic contexts, and incorporating it fluidly into connecting ideas. Here is an example of the phrase played sequentially through the A section of "Star Eyes."

This phrase includes two minor seventh chords, a major third apart.

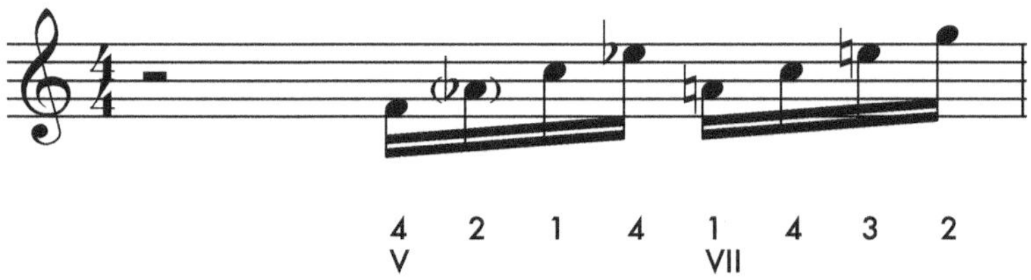

With this device in mind, how could you extend the phrase to explore various ways of moving around the instrument, generating new melodic, rhythmic, and harmonic possibilities? The example below continues the movement of minor seventh arpeggios in major thirds through a wider range.

Line 43

♩ = 133

Source: So What

Line 43 Notes

This line begins with a descending chromatic idea launching from the second finger, starting with a pickup note on the last sixteenth note of beat four.

To study expanding or contracting chromatic lines, launching from different fingers, and the rhythmic consequences of those choices, here is an exercise adding a note to the phrase with each repetition, eventually filling in all four beats of the measure. Count aloud while you play this exercise, staying focused and anticipating the next added note and its rhythmic placement.

While the notation is here as a representation and reference, the challenge and benefit of this exercise will be retaining the figure in your mind and developing awareness of how the phrase changes with each repetition.

This phrase is built from C♯ minor and D minor scalar fragments. Notice how the fingering used facilitates the flow of the idea. When the tonality moves from C♯ minor to D minor, the fingering continues as if the idea were being completed in C♯ but shifts up in position by a half step into D. By using fundamental shapes and fingerings that feel good on the guitar, intricate and harmonically complex language is delivered naturally.

Here is the phrase played without shifting tonalities.

Here is an exercise further exploring how this concept could be applied. It repeats the phrase, retaining the fingering but shifting in different ways. Using phrases and fingerings that you are already comfortable with, try using this technique to navigate to different target tonalities.

Line 44

♩ = 252

Source: Softly, as in a Morning Sunrise

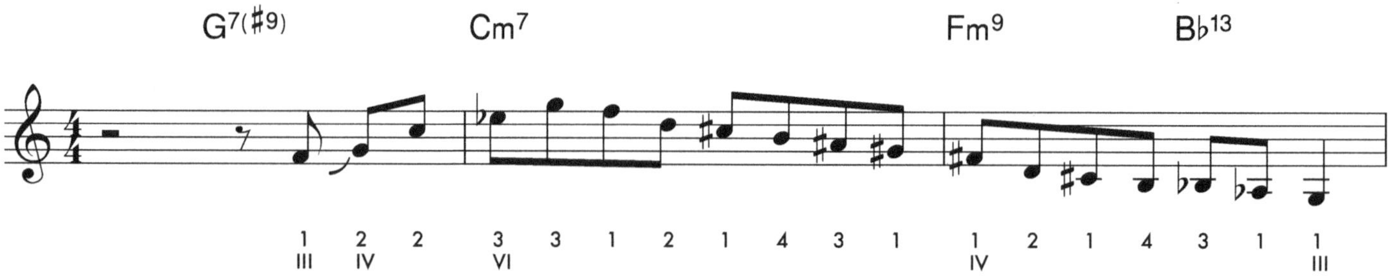

Line 44 Notes

This line begins with an ascending phrase in the C minor tonality, then pivots to a descending phrase in B minor, resolving to E♭ major, anticipating the first chord of the bridge of "Softly, as in a Morning Sunrise."

Try playing ascending phrases up one tonality and down another as an exercise. The example exercise below follows the same pattern as Line 44, ascending in C minor and descending in B minor. For this exercise, C minor phrases are derived from the Dorian mode and B minor phrases from the melodic minor. You could create variations of this exercise using any scale, exploring how to navigate through various tonalities throughout the range of the instrument, with a specific focus on alternating between ascending and descending ideas. For an added challenge and to practice phrases of varying lengths, this exercise begins with four-note phrases, adding one note with each repetition up to eight, then subtracting one note back down to four. (4, 5, 6, 7, 8, 7, 6, 5, 4)

The lines notated above are only an example of how the exercise works. Once you have a sense of alternating between different tonalities and phrase lengths, practice improvising phrases, using the framework presented in the exercise as a limiting/focusing factor. Also, use the principle more loosely, mixed with other language and devices, and applied over various tunes.

Line 45

♩ = 252

Source: Softly, as in a Morning Sunrise

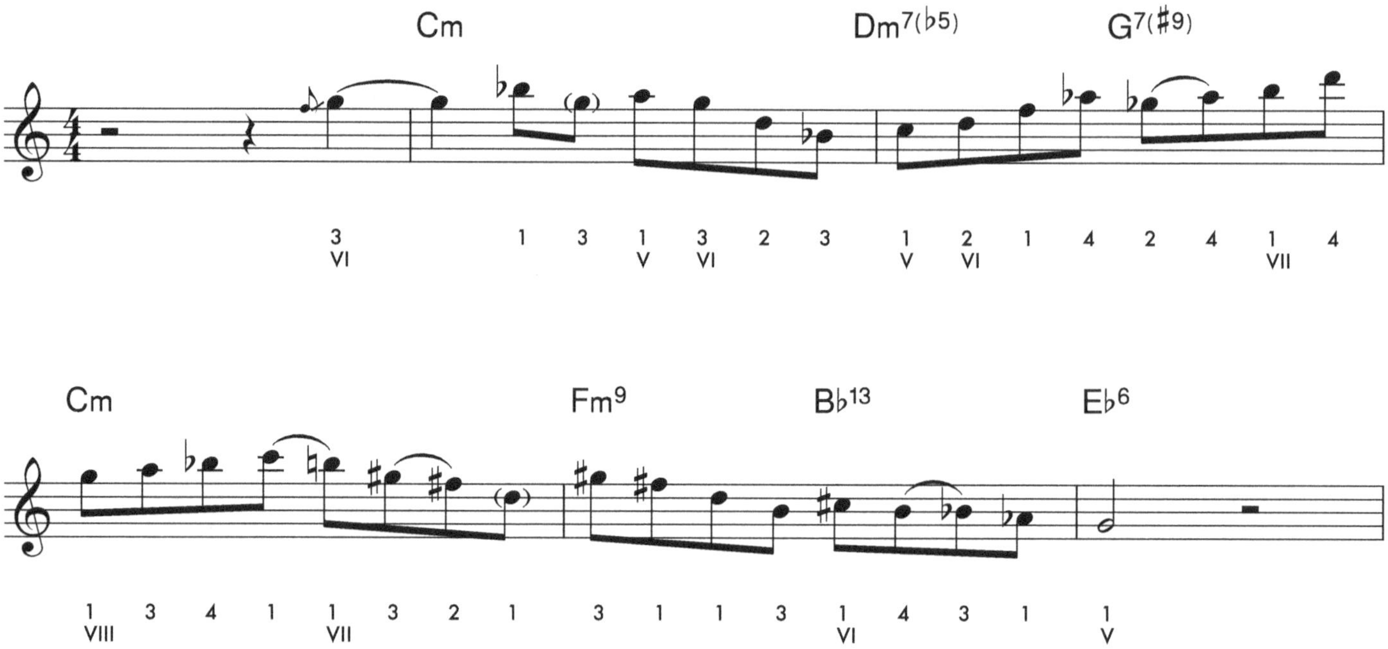

Line 45 Notes

Notice how the first phrase of this line uses a fingering that requires reaching back on the fretboard with your first finger to play a note that is out of position, maintaining the overall posture of all the other fingers involved in playing the phrase. The first finger plays notes on the fifth fret but doesn't "pull" the other fingers with it to play subsequent notes.

Try using this approach with scales and melodic ideas you already know. Here is an example fingering for the G minor pentatonic scale that uses this principle, either reaching down with the first finger or up with the third finger to play notes that are out of position. Experiment with applying this concept, exploring how various ideas sound and feel. Certain types of phrases will work better with this approach than others.

This phrase also utilizes fingerings that require shifting positions. Notice how the four-note cell in the second half of the phrase is played using a fingering likely different from how it would be played if viewed in isolation. However, given the context of where it is coming from, it works perfectly.

To explore this way of moving, here is an exercise using the phrase above, altering only the fifth and sixth notes of the phrase (originally G♭ and A♭). How could other melodic shapes be derived from the same basic physical movement? What are the harmonic consequences of those variations, and how could they be applied?

Line 46

♩ = 220

Source: Unit 7

Line 46 Notes

The first two phrases of this line are derived from the same shape.

The basic shape played in position could be perceived as two sets of fourths a whole tone apart.

As demonstrated in the first phrase of Line 46, the same gesture can generate melodic variations by shifting position midway through the shape.

Here is an exercise using the rhythmic content from Line 46, where the shape is played as a five-note phrase, to get a sense of how the phrase feels, starting on a downbeat and upbeat, and it explores shifting in various ways.

This phrase includes three triads, G minor, G♭ major, and F diminished, each played in a different order (1 5 3) (5 3 1) (3 5 1).

With this in mind, here is an exercise using major triads through the circle of fourths, cycling through the six possible permutations of a major triad with no repeated notes or inversions. The permutations are 135, 153, 315, 351, 513, and 531. The same principle could apply to any triad. Once you get a sense of the exercise, try it with a different type of triad (minor, diminished, augmented), play various permutations through tunes, and improvise with this concept.

Here is an example exercise using the same concept through the first eight bars of "Giant Steps."

Line 47

♩ = 133

Source: Speak Low

Line 47 Notes

This whole line is played in a triplet feel. Notice how the first phrase is grouped rhythmically into twos, marked by a repeating low-high pattern, including ghost notes that are more felt than heard.

Grouping triplets into twos creates an underlying three-over-two rhythmic relationship. Play only the higher notes in the low-high pattern to observe what that ratio feels like when isolated. Count aloud to hear the relationship clearly within the four-beat cycle.

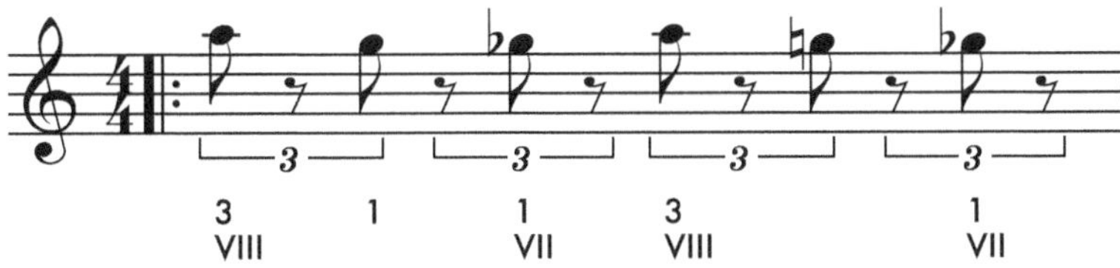

Now play only the lower notes in the low-high pattern. Again, the same three-over-two relationship exists, shifted by one triplet.

Here is an exercise that rotates between playing the isolated high and low notes and the composite phrase. Count aloud for clarity and to develop an awareness of how these parts fit within the beat. For an added challenge, sing a clave pattern while playing the exercise.

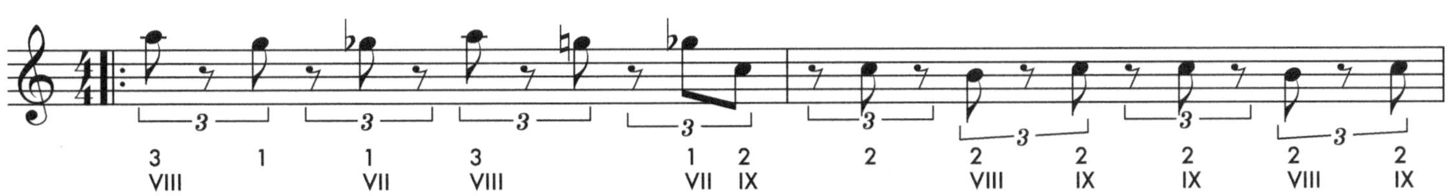

A central feature of the first phrase of this line is how ghost notes foster a type of rhythmic feeling. To work on the mechanics of playing ghost notes, here is an exercise that draws upon the low-high gesture played by skipping strings. There are many different ways of playing ghost notes. Try a range of approaches, from not sounding the note at all (fingering the note with the left hand and moving the right hand as if picking the note without striking the string) to picking the note at a range of dynamic levels, from entirely inaudible to just a bit quieter than the non-ghosted note.

To further explore the feeling of launching phrases from different parts of the beat in a triplet feel, here is an exercise using an excerpt from the line, shifting it through the partials of the triplet. Apply this process to any phrase to better understand how an idea sounds and feels when framed in different ways rhythmically.

Line 48

♩ = 113

Source: Lover Man

Line 48 Notes

This line begins with a G minor tetrachord repeated up an octave. Notice that to retain the same fingering there is a shift in position up two frets.

This type of movement, where a physical shape is repeated throughout the range of the guitar, allows for consistency in how each phrase feels in different octaves. To explore applying this principle to a wider range of the instrument with minor and major tetrachords in various keys, here is an example exercise alternating between minor and major shapes, playing each in three octaves. The exercise uses the rhythm played in Line 48. Since it is a four-note shape played in a sixteenth-note subdivision, starting it off the beat has a less rigid feeling than a pattern that lands on the beat.

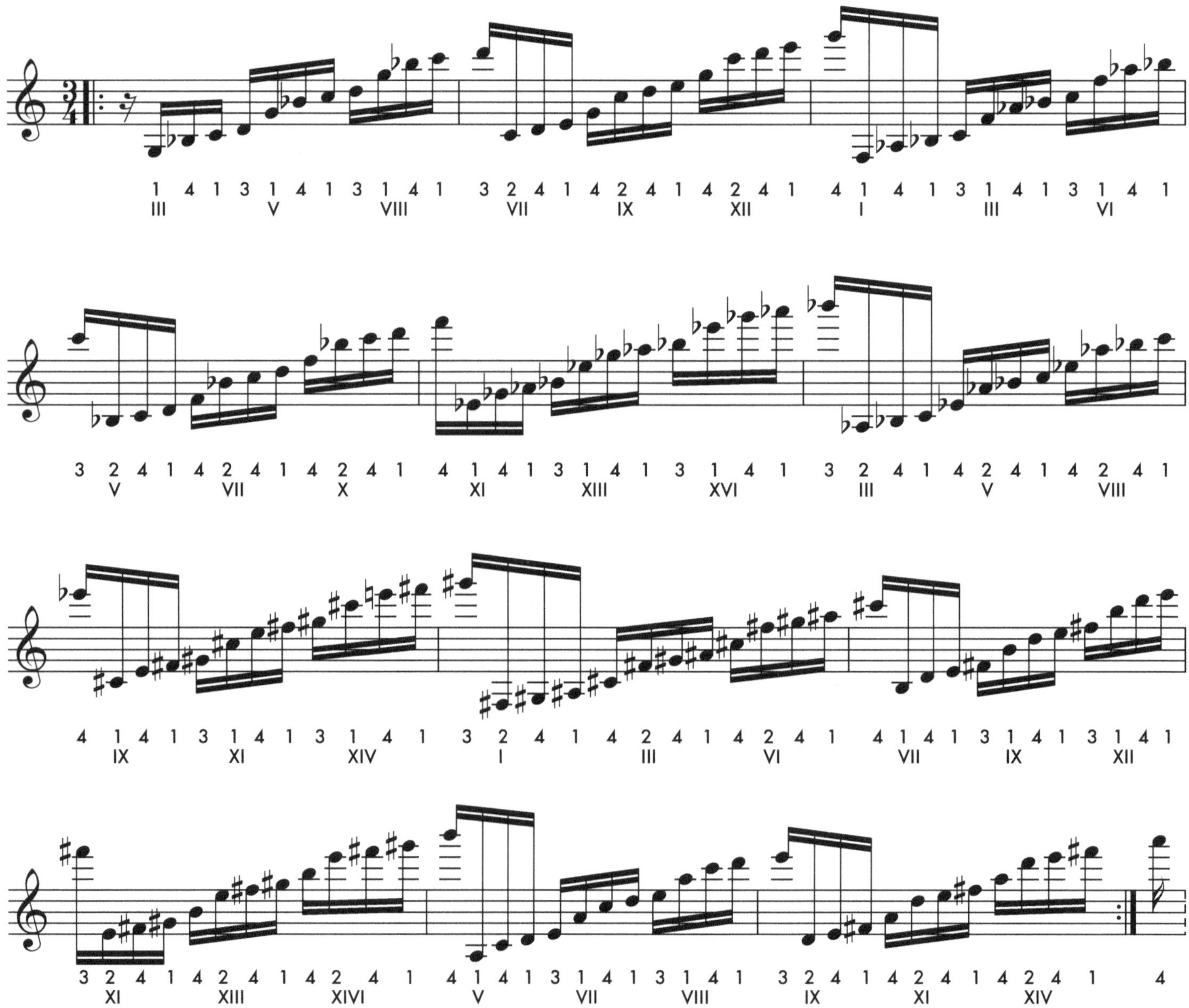

This phrase, all diatonic to the key of F major, could be used as a resource for generating scale exercises built on ascending scalar fragments broken up into various note groupings.

Here is an example exercise based on the first ten notes of this phrase, moving the figure through the F major scale. Try creating variations based on the concept of moving parts of the phrase sequentially through the F major scale. Beyond exercises, apply this concept more loosely in your improvisations, playing ascending scalar passages broken up into various rhythmic lengths and connecting this device to other language and devices you use.

Line 49

♩ = 133

Source: Little Sunflower

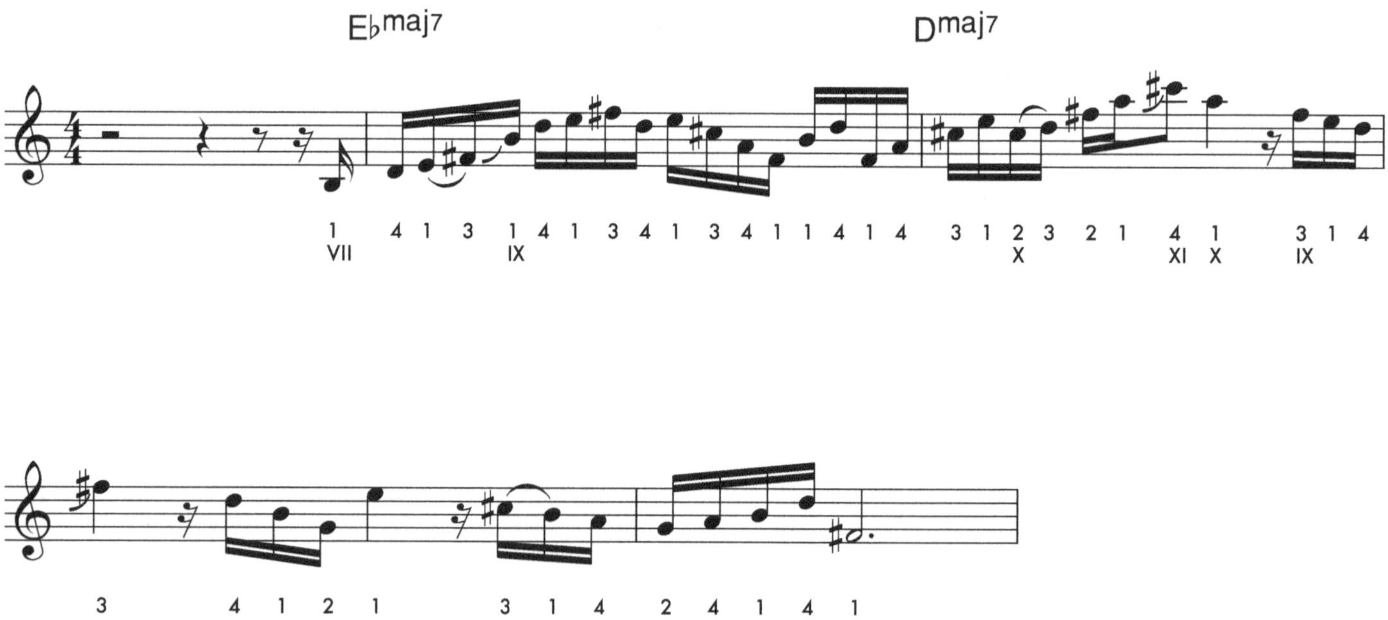

Line 49 Notes

Notice how the last three phrases in this line are built from the same rhythmic idea. The rhythm is repeated in the first and second phrases and extended in the final phrase.

The exercise below generates variations by extending the seed rhythms or melodic ideas, repeating each phrase, and adding a note until it connects with the following phrase. This is an example of one way of working with rhythmic or melodic ideas to derive variations that can expand your ability to use seed material in new ways. Try applying this concept to any phrase you are working with, extending it rhythmically and melodically in various ways, and getting a feeling for how the variations generated connect with other ideas.

Line 50

♩ = 233

Source: Blues in F

Line 50 Notes

This line combines multiple different ways of moving on the instrument. Observe the approaches involved and how the applied principles can provide source material for further exploration.

This phrase begins with a quick shift in position and generally follows the principle of directionalism, moving downward in pitch while moving upward on the guitar neck.

As an exercise, develop variations that utilize the same physical and rhythmic framework, drawing on the overall shape of the original idea but altering it to find new melodic possibilities. Here are some examples of figures that could be generated using this process. Of course, there are countless more possibilities. The benefit of this practice is spending time with the material, trying things, and keeping note of the sounds you discover and how they could be applied.

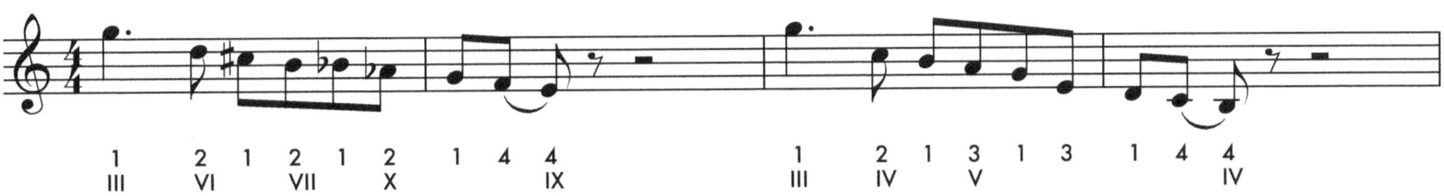

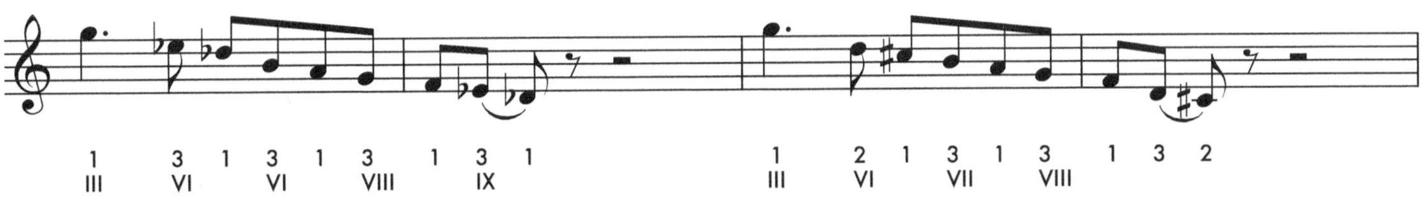

This phrase is built primarily with arpeggios and a descending pentatonic idea. Each section of this phrase is compact and played with a relatively standard fingering. The points of connection, the choices of how to navigate to each section, shifting position at the start of a new arpeggio or sliding into a repeated note, build kinetic energy into the line, creating a distinct feeling of continuous motion.

Try experimenting with different sections of this phrase, altering, recombining, rotating, repeating, or replacing ideas. Here are two examples that use the same arpeggios, Cm7 and B♭maj7, switching their location with each other, leading to different potential descending phrases.

Here is an example using the arpeggios in the original order but reconfiguring the number of notes, borrowing the length from the other arpeggio. So instead of 4+6+4, it is now 6+4+4. The groupings are made clear not only by the pitch selection but also by the fingering used.

Using the same concept, here is an example that reconfigures the note length to 5+5+4.

These examples illustrate the possibilities generated by using your creativity and curiosity. By experimenting, you will find ways of applying these ideas that resonate with you.

Line 51

♩ = 120

Source: D Minor Blues

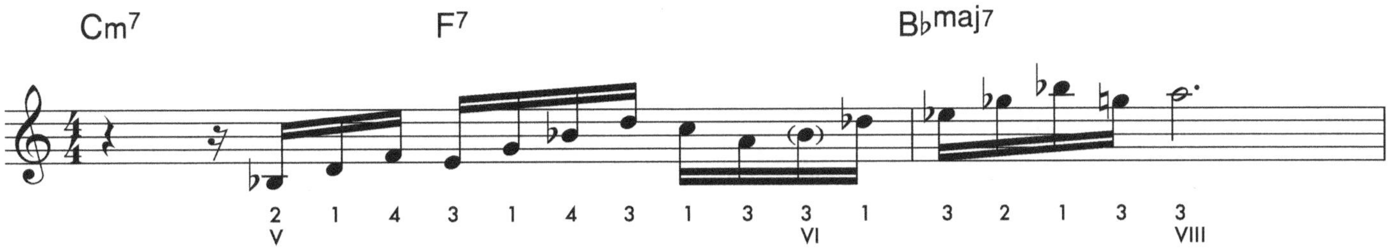

Line 51 Notes

Notice how this phrase includes arpeggios of differing lengths derived from the B♭ Lydian scale (or, depending on your perception, any mode with the same pitches). The phrase consists of three arpeggios, each with a different number of notes (3+4+2). A change in direction marks each new shape.

Here is an exercise that retains the direction of each arpeggio through the scale but alters the number of notes, moving through different possible permutations of the source phrase.

This phrase momentarily pivots to the E♭ minor tonality, delaying the resolution to B♭ major.

Here is an exercise that explores delaying the resolution further, pushing it by one note with each repetition, and generating a rhythmic practice targeting different parts of the beat. Count aloud.

Line 52

♩ = 264 Source: Blues Minor

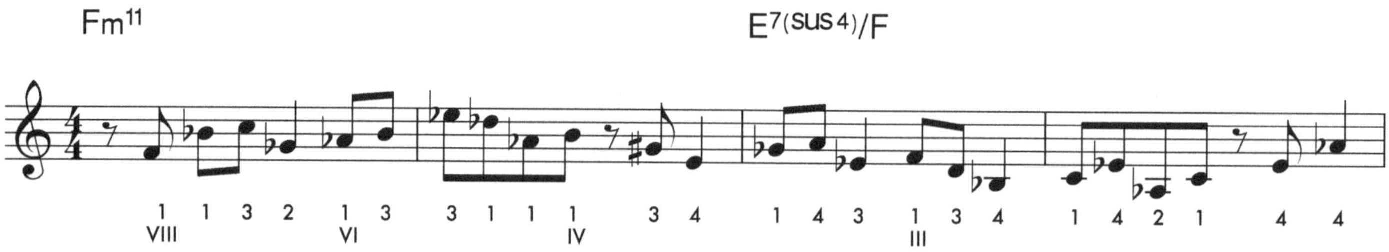

Line 52 Notes

This line could be perceived as three distinct musical sentences. Compact shapes, precise rhythmic gestures, and punctuation create structure within each sentence. Individually, each stands on its own in terms of having a compelling beginning, middle, and end. Together, they form a complete musical statement. Here are the three sentences broken up visually to contemplate them in a different way. The inner structure of each sentence is made clear by shifts in position, tonality, or rhythm.

As a practice, contemplate each sentence. Loop a sentence to meditate on how the cells work together to form the larger idea. Play the sentences in different feels and tempos. Try adjusting dynamics. Repeat individual cells, and try expanding or altering cells and connecting them in new ways. There are numerous ways of looking at each of these shapes. Use the ideas suggested here as a starting point for experimentation, then keep working to generate variations based on the material.

This phrase draws on two melodic shapes, a major triad, and a major tetrachord, generated from tonalities a tritone apart, B♭ major and E major.

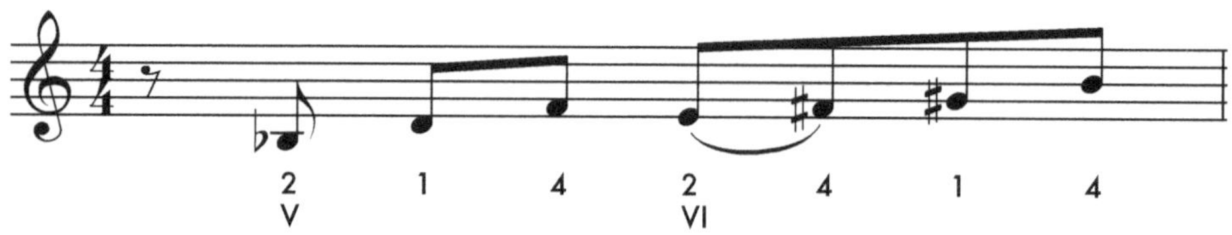

Here are some exercises based on the tritone relationship, using the major triad and tetrachord and combining them in different ways through a wider range of the instrument.

2 4 1 4 2 1 4 2 4 1 4 1 1 4 2 4 1 4 2 1 4 4 1 4
V VI VII IX X XVI X
2 4 1 1 4 1 4 2 4 1 2 4 1 4 2 2 3 0
IX VII VI V II

Line 53

♩ = 133

Source: Little Sunflower

Line 53 Notes

Notice how an underlying four-over-three polyrhythm is created by phrasing in groups of three in a sixteenth note subdivision. The groupings are marked by three-note melodic figures that move from high to low.

A four-note figure fills out the remaining space in the bar, creating a 3+3+3+3+4 rhythmic pattern.

With this in mind, consider the other possible ways of breaking up phrases in a bar of 4/4 using the same numbers, 3+3+3+3+4, ordering them in different ways. Here is an example exercise that alters the phrase to reflect the different possible groupings.

(3+3+3+3+4) (3+3+3+4+3)

(3+3+4+3+3) (3+4+3+3+3)

(4+3+3+3+3)

This section of the line is a whole-tone device.

Work out the device through a wider range of the instrument as an exercise.

Here are some variations of the device using the same three-note shape, moving it through the whole-tone scale in several ways. Other potential fingerings work well with these sequences. First, try the notated option, then explore other possibilities.

Line 54

♩ = 258 | Source: Impressions

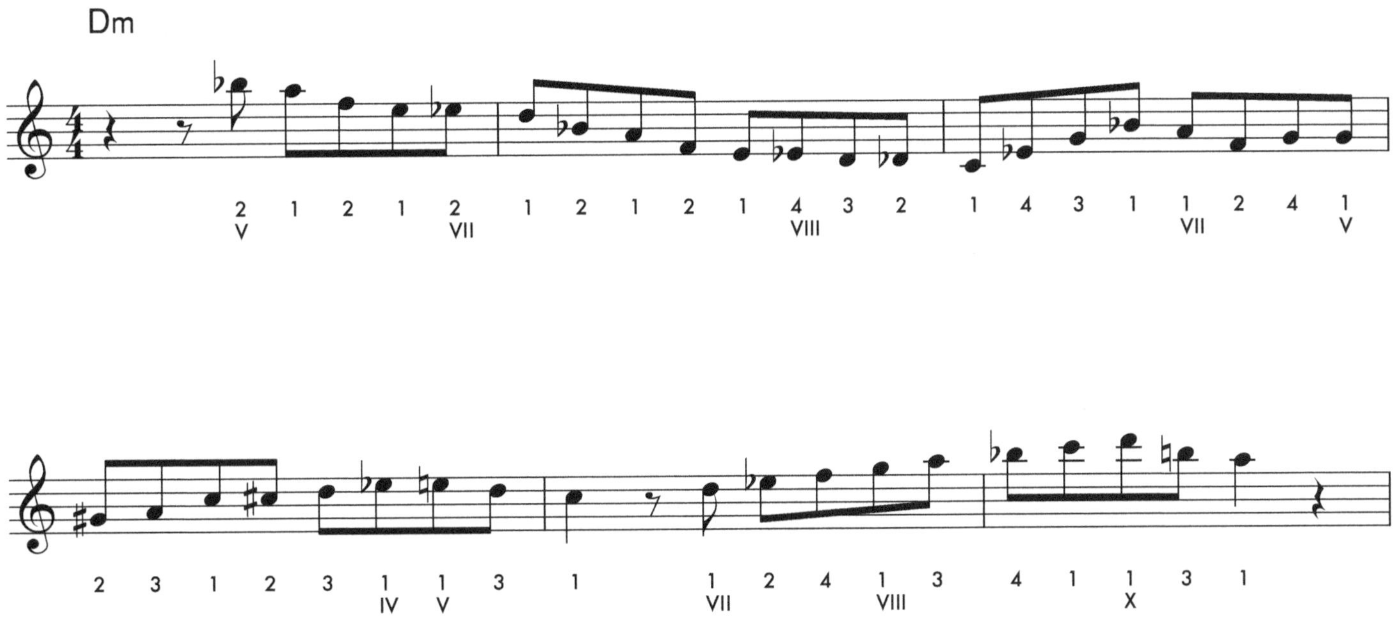

Line 54 Notes

This line begins with a device using two notes per string, chromatic cells, leading into a longer descending chromatic. Notice that the phrase starts on an upbeat, and the number of notes per string is always an even number, two or four. The way that each cell feels rhythmically remains consistent, with finger two on an upbeat and finger one on a downbeat.

Practice creating variations using chromatic cells drawing on the principle of an even number of notes per string. Here are some example variations that use the phrase as a frame, extending the phrase by two notes with each repetition.

Notice how in this phrase, G is repeated on two different strings. Repeating a single pitch on two strings subtly affects timbre and rhythm. Also, by repeating the same note in two different locations or positions on the guitar, the options for where a line can go are expanded into new territory.

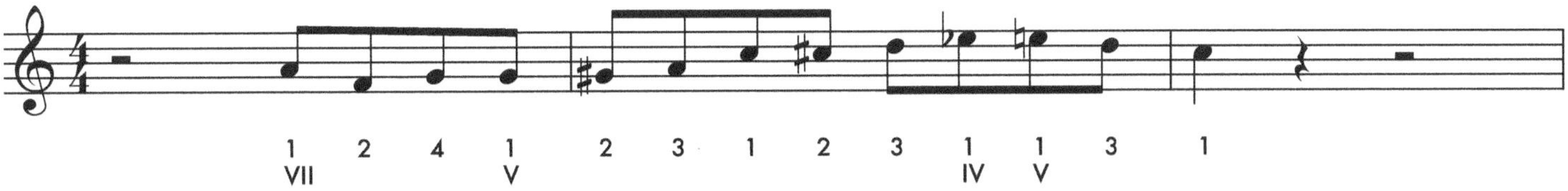

As an exercise, consider other applications of repeated notes to this phrase and the consequences and opportunities created by various approaches. The variations below add a repeated note at different points in the phrase. Explore extending the ideas based on the new directions created by each choice.

Line 55

♩ = 131

Source: Summertime

Line 55 Notes

This phrase is an example of how having a clear sense of direction and target points can allow for the introduction of pitch choices that seemingly clash with the tonality, in this case, D minor. Convincing rhythmic delivery and the rate at which passing tones go by allow for flexibility in pitch selection.

Part of the power of the idea is in how familiar it sounds, giving the impression of a more common phrase and utilizing its physical and rhythmic frame while circumventing conventionality. Here is a more common manifestation of the phrase. Try repeating the phrase, alternating between the two variations. How do the different approaches affect the feeling and intention of the idea?

This chromatic enclosure is a valuable device for connecting phrases in many ways.

Practice incorporating this device into your improvisations, using it as connective tissue leading to various phrases. Here are some example variations that each create different harmonic implications. These illustrate a potential process of working through possibilities. Generate more variations, and practice extending them into more complete phrases. Many alternate fingerings work well for these examples. Try out different options and practice them in different octaves and positions to get a fuller sense of how these could be applied spontaneously.

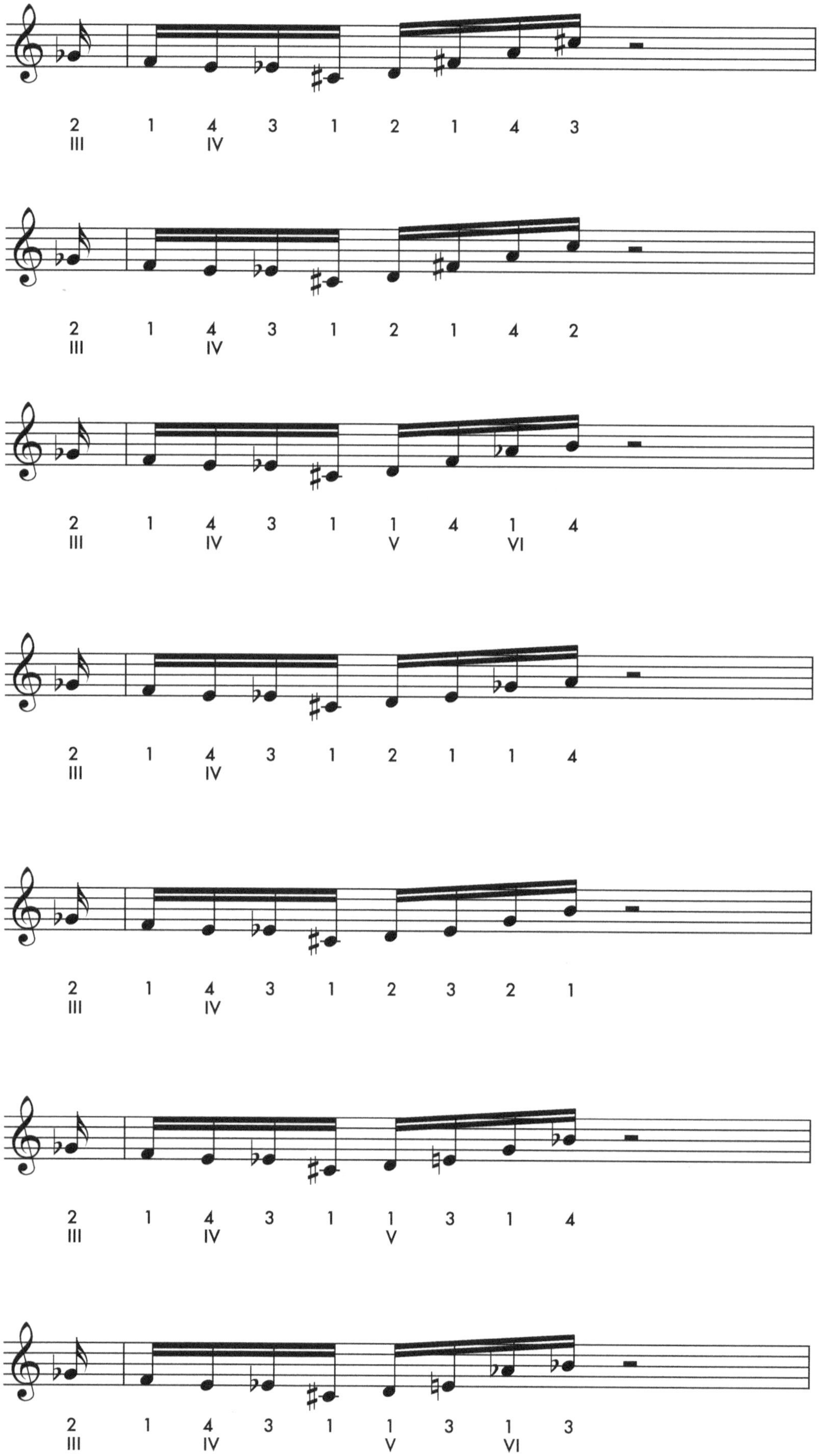
2 1 4 3 1 2 1 4 3
III IV
2 1 4 3 1 2 1 4 2
III IV
2 1 4 3 1 1 4 1 4
III IV V VI
2 1 4 3 1 2 1 1 4
III IV
2 1 4 3 1 2 3 2 1
III IV
2 1 4 3 1 1 3 1 4
III IV V
2 1 4 3 1 1 3 1 3
III IV V VI

Line 56

♩ = 272 | Source: Speak Low

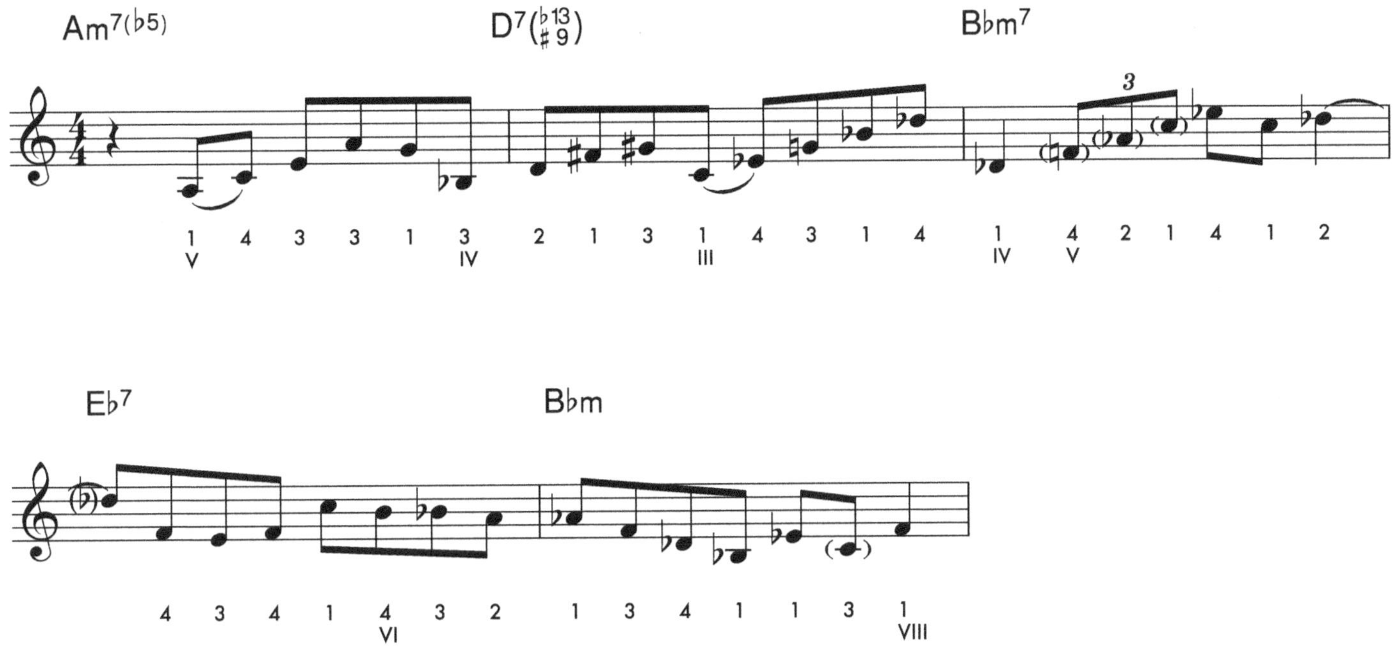

Line 56 Notes

The first phrase of this line is a series of arpeggios with note groupings of five, four, and five. Notice that while the movement of the arpeggios is trending upward, with the lowest note moving from A to B♭ to C, the position in which each arpeggio is played is trending lower on the guitar neck.

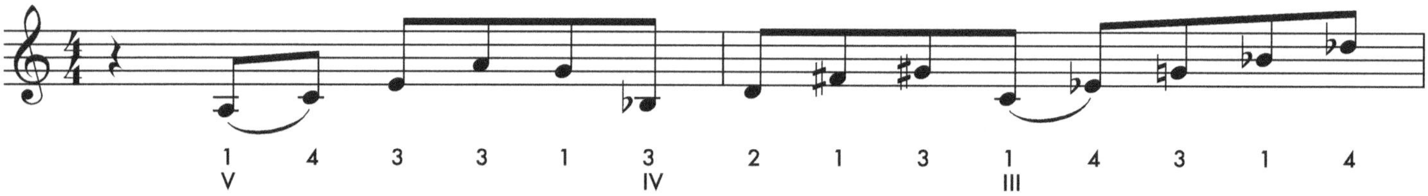

As an exercise, practice rotating the note groupings of the arpeggios to experiment with breaking up the phrase in different ways. The permutations are 5+4+5, 5+5+4, and 4+5+5. Here are some examples of how this could be applied, following the same bass movement while adjusting the number of notes in each arpeggio based on the different patterns.

(5+4+5)

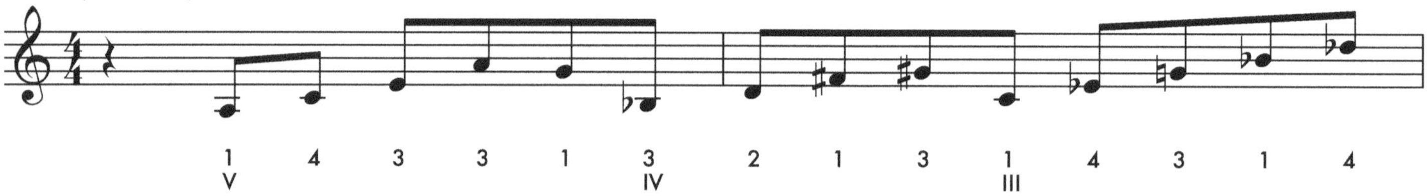

(5+5+4)

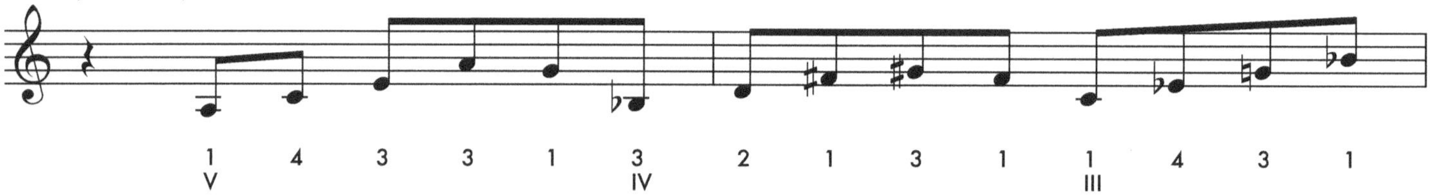

(4+5+5)

Continuing this thought process, consider other ways that the total number of notes in the phrase (14) could be broken up into arpeggios of various note groupings. Here are some more examples.

(7+7) or (4+3+4+3)

(4+3+3+4)

(3+4+4+3)

This phrase is core language frequently applied in the context of a ii V progression, here B♭-7 and E♭7. Practice this in all twelve keys and different positions on the guitar, and explore connecting it with other ideas.

Line 57

♩ = 272

Source: Speak Low

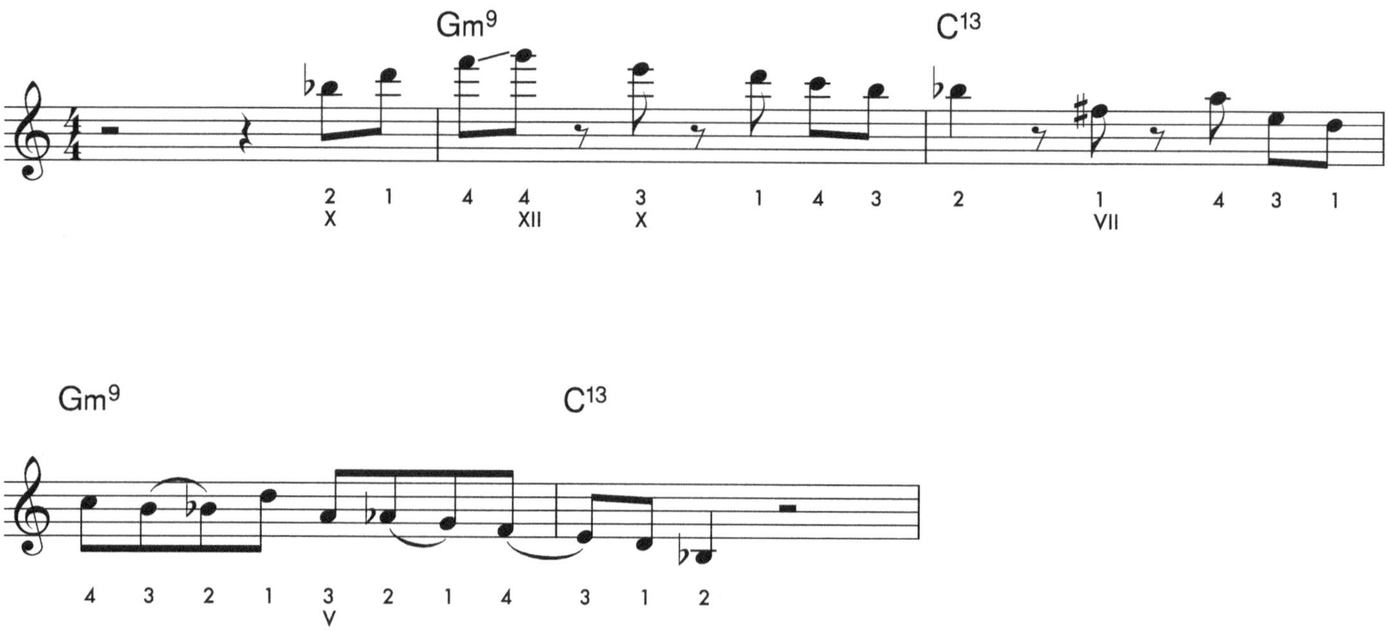

Line 57 Notes

Three moments in this line utilize descending chromatics into a chord tone.

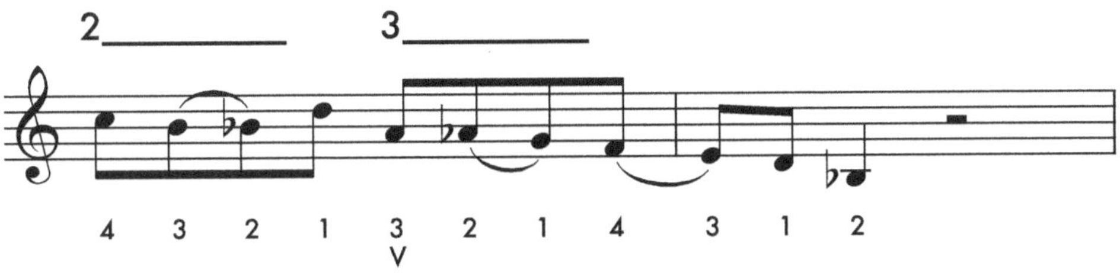

As an exercise, practice targeting all the chord tones of any given chord using the device illustrated in the line. Here is the device applied on two example chords.

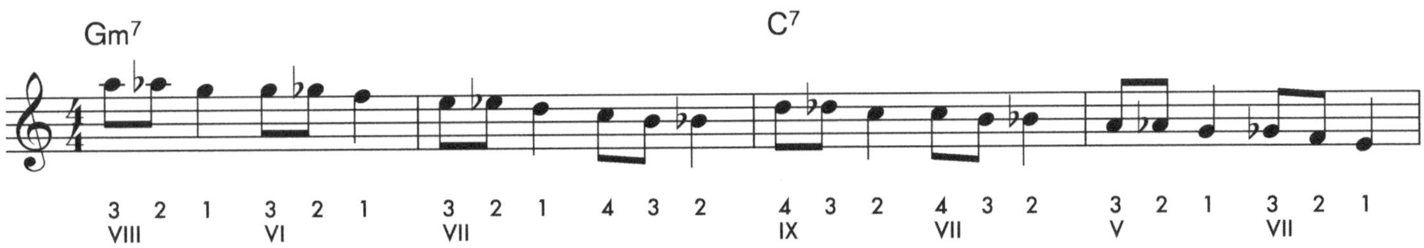

Consider possible ways this simple device could be expanded into longer melodic figures. To start, add a given scale tone above the target chord tone. Here are some examples of this concept, adding a scale tone, a third or a fifth above the target chord tone.

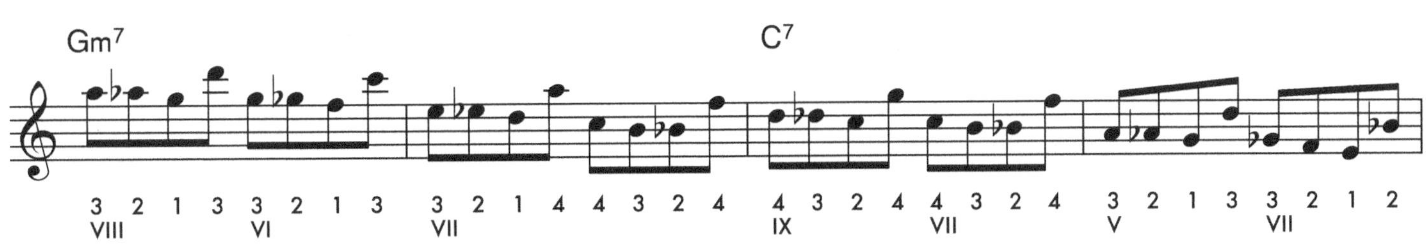

In the previous examples, the added tone is diatonic to the scale. Also, apply the concept purely on an intervallic basis (major third, minor third, diminished fifth, etc.), resulting in some tones outside the scale and yielding different transpositions of the same shape. Here is an example using major thirds.

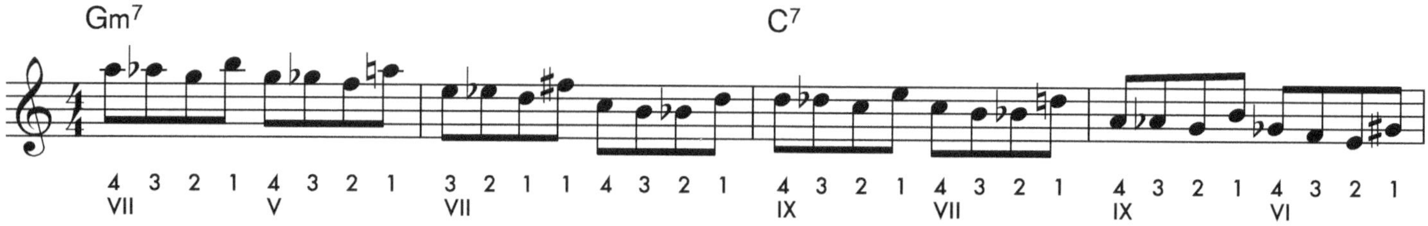

Here are some additional examples extending the device to create five-note and six-note cells using scale tones.

Extend the device as far as your imagination allows. Once you have worked through some of the example variations above, generate your own. Apply the concept in your improvisations on tunes, incorporating it into your existing language.

Applying both the basic device and expanded figures requires a strong foundation in terms of chords. If finding the chord tones in a given chord is slowing you down, work on the fundamentals, memorizing chords and arpeggios throughout the range of the instrument.

Line 58

♩ = 220

Source: Blues in F

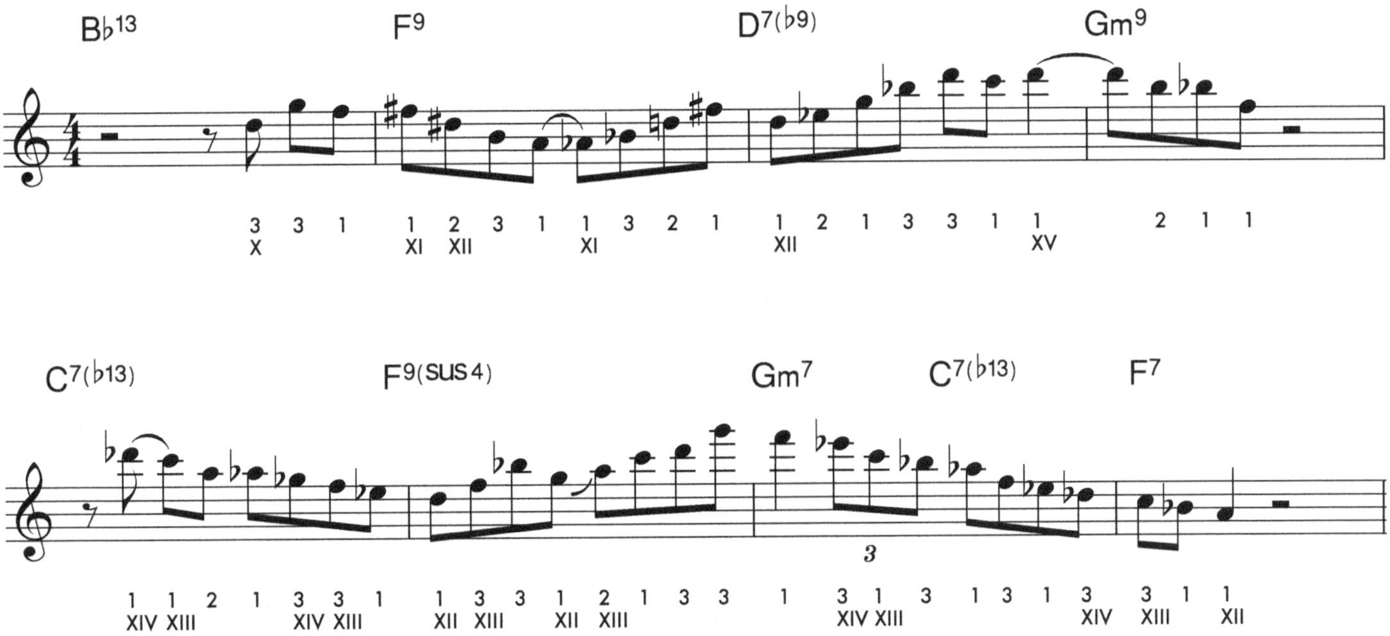

Line 58 Notes

This line is played with a three-finger technique, using fingers one, two, and three, and not using the pinky. Some guitarists use this technique as their core approach to the instrument. Generally, this applies to single-note lines, with most guitarists using four fingers (and sometimes five, including the thumb on the left hand) for chords.

Because the pinky is inherently the weakest finger, this technique takes advantage of the natural strength of the first three fingers. As a result, it can positively impact the feeling and consistency of sound when playing lines. Using this approach can also subtly affect the duration of notes since the hand has to move more horizontally on the neck.

Try alternating between three and four-finger techniques, repeating phrases, and observing the differences. Here is an example exercise, looping the first phrase of Line 58, alternating between the different fingerings.

Another subtle mechanical choice is playing a repeated note on the same string with a different finger. Notice how in this phrase, the high D is first played with the third finger and then repeated with the first finger, requiring a shift in position, opening up new territory on the guitar and impacting the rest of the phrase.

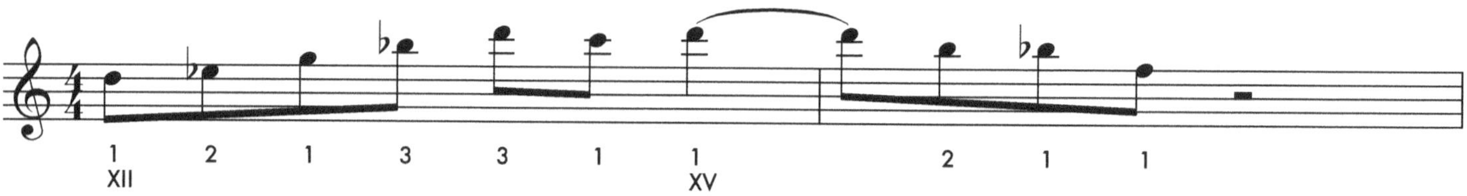

As an exercise, play a simple scale pattern using a different finger for each repetition of the same note. In addition to the notated fingering in this example, experiment with alternative finger combinations and explore the sonic and mechanical impact of different approaches.

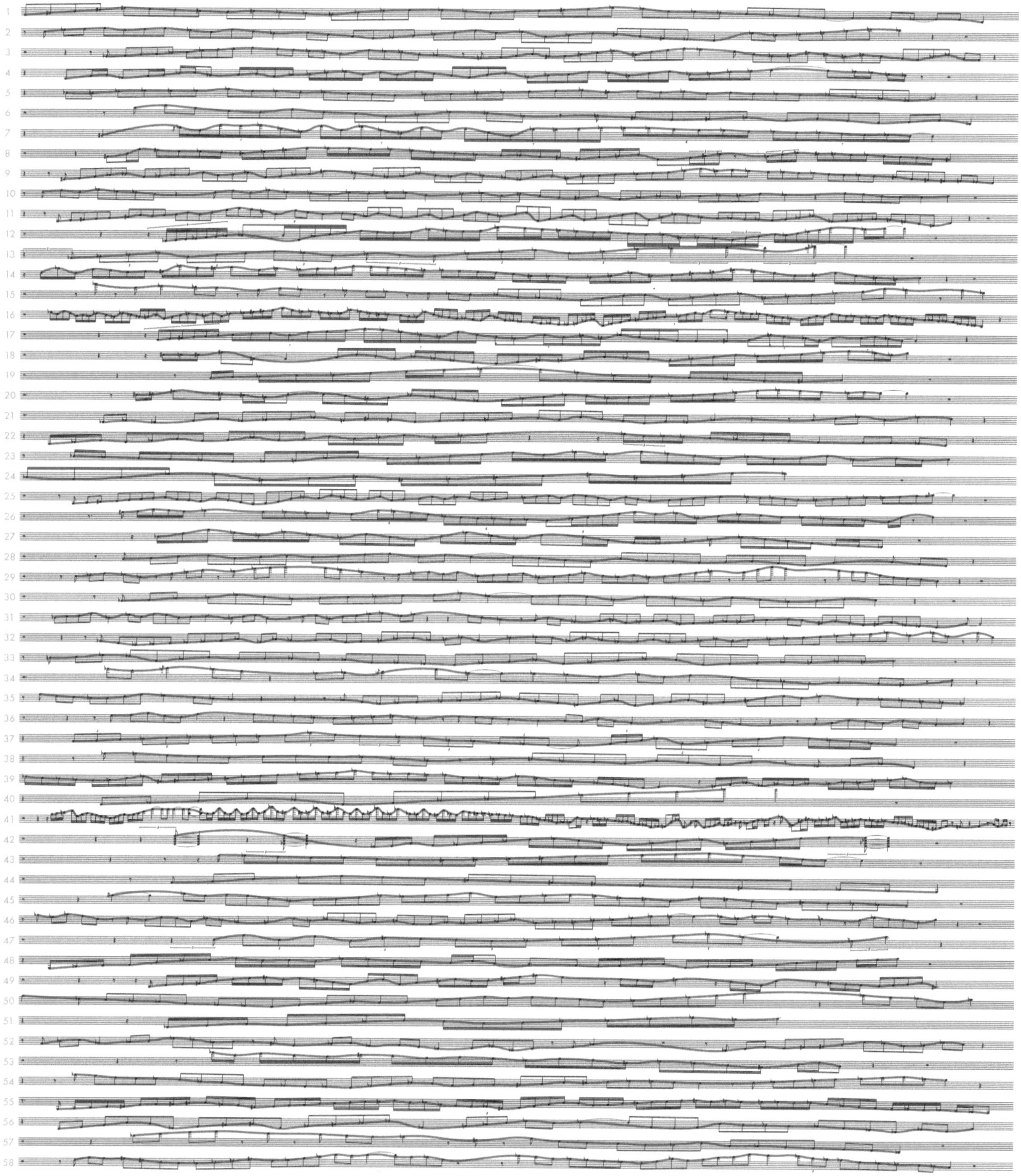

RODNEY JONES

"Rodney Jones is a legend among musicians, especially guitarists. He is worthy of the ears of any music listener." - George Benson

Rodney Jones is at the leading edge of modern jazz guitar, extending the rhythmic, linear, and harmonic possibilities of the instrument while being firmly rooted in the tradition. Rodney started playing the guitar at age six. He has recorded two records for the Blue Note label, *The Undiscovered Few* and *Soul Manifesto*. He has toured worldwide, and performed and recorded with a who's who of music, including Dizzy Gillespie, James Brown, Lena Horne, Quincy Jones, Christian McBride, Stevie Wonder, Elvin Jones, Kenny Burrell, Stan Getz, and countless others. He was the house guitarist for the Apollo Theatre for nine years and the staff guitarist for the Rosie O'Donnell Show for six years. He has written commercials, and has more than 125 compositions recorded. He recently scored a documentary film for PBS about African American GIs in WW2. He served as Musical Director/Producer for Lena Horne, Ruth Brown, Gloria Lynne, Ernestine Anderson, and others. He has been a professor of Jazz Guitar Studies at The Juilliard School for 12 years and The Manhattan School of Music for more than 20 years and has conducted clinics and workshops worldwide.

OTHER MEL BAY JAZZ GUITAR IMPROVISATION BOOKS

Hip Guitar Lines (Rodney Jones)
Outside Sounds and Substitutions for Modern Jazz Guitar (K. Miller)
Advanced Jazz Guitar Improvisation (B. Greene)
Advanced Rhythmic Concepts for Improvisation (Allen)
All Blues for Jazz Guitar (Ferguson)
All Blues Scale for Jazz Guitar (Ferguson)
All Blues Soloing for Jazz Guitar (Ferguson)
All Intros & Endings for Jazz Guitar (Ferguson)
Arpeggios for the Evolving Guitarist (Pat Kelley)
Complete Book of Jazz Guitar Lines & Phrases (Jacobs)
Complete Book of Jazz Single String Studies (Salvador)
Complete Guitar Improvisation Book (Bredice)
Double-Symmetrical Augmented Scale for Jazz Improvisation (Oro)
Essential Jazz Lines in the Style of Joe Pass (C. Christiansen)
Essential Jazz Lines in the Style of Grant Green (C. Christiansen)
Essential Jazz Lines in the Style of Wes Montgomery (C. Christiansen)
Extreme Warm-Ups and Chops Builders for Guitar (Anthony)
Fingerboard Mastery Book One USC Curriculum (Potenza and Stoubis)
Fingerboard Mastery Book Two USC Curriculum (Potenza and Stoubis)
Frank Vignola's Complete Jammin' The Blues Play-Along for Guitar
Frank Vignola's Complete Rhythm Changes Play-Along for Guitar
Fundamentals of Guitar (Miles Okazaki)
Getting Your Improvising into Shape (Becker)
Guitar Arpeggio Studies on Jazz Standards (Mimi Fox)
Graduated Soloing (Mimi Fox)
Improvisational Techniques for Jazz Guitar (Umble)
Improvising with Mini-Arpeggios (Musso)
Into the Labyrinth (Mooney)
Personalizing Jazz Vocabulary (Mooney)
Jazz Blues Styles (Diorio)
Jazz Course for All Instruments (Gabric)
Jazz Intros and Endings (Eschette)
Jazz Guitar Essentials: Gig Savers Complete Edition (C. Christiansen)
Jazz Guitar Lines Workout (C. Christiansen)
Jazz Guitar Phrasing Workout (W. Bay)
Jazz Guitar Structures (Andrew Green)
Jazz Guitar Technique (Andrew Green)
Jazz Guitar Wall Chart (C. Christiansen)
Jazz Pentatonics (Saunders)
Jazz Scale Workout (Karsh)
Jazz Scales for Guitar (C. Christiansen)